Christ the Center

DIETRICH BONHOEFFER

Christ The Center

INTRODUCED BY
EDWIN H. ROBERTSON
AND
TRANSLATED BY
JOHN BOWDEN

HARPER & ROW, PUBLISHERS
New York

Contents

CONTENTS

Bonhoeffer's Christology

by

Edwin H. Robertson

Bonhœffer's Christology

The popular conception of Bonhœffer is of a theologian
who would have done with all the religious elements of the
church and perhaps even with the church itself. As a radical
theologian, he is not thought of as one who gets to the root
of the matter, as the word would imply, but as an iconoclast.
There are certainly many sentences in his *Letters and Papers
from Prison* which, when quoted out of context, give credence
to this view. Yet he was and remained a Lutheran and a
very orthodox churchman. His last act before he died was
to conduct a religious service, and there are many points
in the closing letters that indicate his unwillingness to be
too radical. To quote but one: *3rd August 1944*, 'I am often
shocked at the things I am saying, especially in the first
part [i.e. of his theological work and with special reference
to a chapter on "Taking Stock of Religion"], which is
mainly critical. I shall be glad when I get to the more
positive part. But the whole subject has never been properly
thrashed out, so it sounds very undigested. However, ·it
can't be printed at present and will doubtless improve
with waiting.'[1]

The more positive side, which was never written down,
can only be recovered by study of his earlier writings, and
it is for this reason that the publishers have tried to give the
English-speaking public as much Bonhœffer in English as
possible. Quite clearly, not everything that Bonhœffer
wrote was good, but almost all he wrote helps us to recon-

[1] *Letters and Papers from Prison*, Fontana Books, 1959, p. 131.

struct the positive side of his thinking at a time when only
the negative appears to be known. Of course, there must
be selection, and this small book which contains reconstructed lectures given by Bonhœffer in 1933 on the theme
of christology needs justifying. There are two obstacles to
be overcome.

First, this is not Bonhœffer's text—it has been reconstructed from notes by his students. With so much genuine
Bonhœffer material still not translated, why pick on this
doubtful text? The answer is that christology is at the heart
of Bonhœffer's theology and that Eberhard Bethge is better
qualified than any man living to reconstruct what Bonhœffer really said. Here we can listen to Bonhœffer, not
talking about Bonhœffer's contribution to christology, but
Bonhœffer lecturing on christology and making his contribution incidentally. There is much in these lectures that
we should expect to find in any lectures on christology, but
through an examination of this material we come very close
to the mind of Bonhœffer. The question he is answering is
not, 'What do you think of Christ?', a question he would
have rejected; but, 'How has Christ been understood and
what is wrong with the classical concepts of christology?'
There are many reasons why we need to understand 'Bonhœffer's christology' if we are to understand what he
intended to write in a positive way about the church in his
chapter on 'Taking Stock of Religion'. Some of these will
be given later.

Meanwhile, a second objection is that this series of
lectures was given in 1933. This is an early date, before
most of the great events in Bonhœffer's life had taken shape,
and before he had matured his thought about the church.
Our scientific way of thinking has accustomed us to discount
what is old and read only the new. This is unwise in
philosophy or theology. Certainly, the later writings are a

development of the earlier and have taken into account the impact of later events and the fruit of much further thought. But a theologian will often assume what he has already written and leave his later writings to add to his earlier rather than replace them. There is clear evidence that Bonhœffer is one of these. In a letter he wrote after the failure of the July plot in 1944, he questions his famous book, *The Cost of Discipleship*, with words that are significant: 'I thought I could acquire faith by trying to live a holy life, or something like it. It was in this phase that I wrote *The Cost of Discipleship*. Today I can see the dangers of this book, though,' he adds, 'I am prepared to stand by what I wrote.'[1] Later, as he explains in that letter, he learnt that only by living in this world completely could he acquire faith. What he had written in 1937 might have to be modified, but not cancelled. He still sees holiness as a way to faith, but now it is 'worldly holiness'.

Bonhœffer's attitude to christology in 1933 was not annulled by later thought or experience. It remained the basis of his thinking about Christ. If today we are to understand what he meant by the church it is essential to read these lectures, and even then they are incomplete, for Bonhœffer never finished the course. Like some of Leonardo da Vinci's works, they tell us much and make us long for more. At least we have as much as his students had. Martin E. Marty, in his introduction to the chapter on the lectures in *The Place of Bonhœffer*,[2] writes of them: 'In the four-volume Collected Works, no single piece can compete for interest and importance with Bethge's recomposition of these lectures from students' notes'; and the author of the chapter itself, Jaroslav Pelikan, says, 'This is one of the most positive essays in the book.' I would strongly recom-

[1] *Letters and Papers from Prison*, p. 125.
[2] SCM Press, 1963, p. 143.

mend that admirable chapter[1] as a commentary on Bonhœffer's christology. It alone would be enough to justify
the translation of these lectures into English, and their
publication as a major event in the presentation of the
thinking of Bonhœffer to the English-speaking world.
Neither the date, nor the unfinished state of the text should
keep us from giving very careful attention to what they
contain.

Having disposed of the two possible objections, it might
be well to look at the positive reasons for putting this text
into English. Some have already been indicated. The main
reason is the importance of the subject—at any period in
his life, christology is the key to Bonhœffer's thought. This
is evident in the way he deals with his most radical problems.
At the Berlin Youth Conference in April 1932, the young
Bonhœffer denounced the appeal to 'orders of creation' in
a discussion of war and peace. He saw the danger of
declaring that anything was good because it was made good.
The appeal to Genesis I, with which he had just been
wrestling in the lectures that later became *Creation and Fall*,
seemed to him specious and dangerous. When God declared
creation 'very good', he spoke of an unspoiled creation and
not the world we know. For 'orders of creation' he sub-
stituted 'orders of preservation'. In writing up this discussion in a report for *Die Eiche*, Bonhœffer explained the
difference: 'The difference was that in the light of the
concept of orders of creation, ordinances and features of the
world were regarded as valuable, original, "very good"
in themselves, whereas the concept of orders of preservation
meant that each feature was only a feature preserved by
God, in grace and anger, in view of the revelation of Christ.
Any order under the preservation of God was set and
directed by Christ and only preserved for his sake. An

[1] *The Place of Bonhœffer*, pp. 145-64.

order is only to be regarded as an order of preservation so long as it is still open for the proclamation of the Gospel. Where an order is basically closed to this proclamation, be it apparently the most original—marriage, nation, etc.—it must be surrendered. The solution of general ethical problems . . . must be sought only in the revelation of God in Christ, and not from orders of creation.'[1]

Already in 1930, in his inaugural lecture which had man as its theme, 'Man in Contemporary Philosophy and Theology', he summarised his survey of the treatment of 'man' in terms of christology. The key passage has been quoted by Dr. Pelikan in his own translation.[2] I would prefer to use my own translation, from *No Rusty Swords*, not because of any basic disagreement but because I prefer the solution John Bowden and I found to the insoluble problem of the translation of *'Gemeinde'* to the equally valid translation used by Dr. Pelikan. Whatever *Gemeinde* does mean in this context, both of us have recognised that it does not mean 'congregation'. I hope Dr. Pelikan will forgive me for using church more sparingly than he does, and at times translating it with the preferred Bonhœffer concept of 'community'. The passage is as follows: 'It is the mystery of the community that Christ is in her and, only through her, reaches to men. Christ exists among us as community, as church in the hiddenness of history. The church is the hidden Christ among us. Now therefore man is never alone, but he exists only through the community which brings him Christ, which incorporates him in itself, takes him into its life. Man in Christ is man in community; where he exists is community. But because at the same time as individual he is fully a member of the community, therefore here alone is the continuity of his existence preserved in

---

[1] *No Rusty Swords*, Harper & Row, 1965, p. 180.
[2] *The Place of Bonhœffer*, p. 146.

Christ. Therefore man can no longer understand himself from himself, but only from Christ.'[1]

It was a straight line of development from this early inaugural lecture to the draft of his major work on Ethics, still unfinished at the end.[2] In that, he rejected the 'formation' that sought to impose morality from without, but built his new morality upon a renewal of the mind from within. This process of renewal, with no outward forces trying to impose an alien pattern on the mind but rather an inherent growth shaping the mind until man becomes what he is, was seen as the growth of the mind to be like that of Christ. This was more than the 'imitation of Christ'; it meant the power of Christ working within until man becomes fully human—Christlike, because that is what man is intended to be. All else is less than human. And so humanity again depends for its authenticity on Christ.

Before turning to the lectures themselves and the events of the year in which they were given, I should like to consider a letter which Bonhœffer wrote to his friend on the 8th June 1944.[3] Eberhard Bethge had obviously asked a series of theological questions which were troubling him and apparently also Bonhœffer. The answer he gets is not the crystal clear reply of a theologian, but the puzzling response of an honest and not yet clear believer. The only thing Bonhœffer feels absolutely sure of is his attitude to Christ. Of the questions, he says, 'I should be happy if I could answer them all myself,' and goes on, in a passage which shows his real genius and the reason why his letters continue to be read by men who still seek answers to the fundamental questions: 'I am led on more by an instinctive feeling for the questions which are bound to crop up than by any conclusions I have reached already.' There follows

[1] *No Rusty Swords*, p. 68.   [2] *Ethics*, Fontana Library, 1965.
[3] *Letters and Papers from Prison*, pp. 106-10.

a brilliant analysis of the failure of contemporary theologians to realise the full seriousness of the questions being raised. In a historical preamble he traces the impact of the Renaissance—giving the 13th century as his estimated date when this movement towards the autonomy of man had reached a measure of completeness. Since then, he claims, 'Man has learnt to cope with all questions of importance without recourse to God as a working hypothesis.' And so, 'what we call "God" is being more and more edged out of life.' The world becomes sure of itself and the church gets more and more frightened. Then it makes the mistake of trying to bring in God and Christ to counter this trend. That makes the movement towards autonomy anti-Christian. The fatal mistake of the church was to try and 'prove to a world come of age that it cannot live without the tutelage of "God".' The inability to maintain this in the face of the world's autonomy leads to the 'ultimate questions', where God now takes refuge. Here at least he is needed.

At this point comes Bonhœffer's most quoted question, a rhetorical one: 'But what if one day they [i.e. these ultimate questions] no longer exist as such, if they too can be answered without "God"?' Bonhœffer shrewdly points out that secular equivalents to religion play the same game. These are the existentialist philosophers and the psychiatrists who 'demonstrate to secure, contented, happy mankind that he is really unhappy and desperate and merely unwilling to realise that he is in severe straits he knows nothing at all about, from which they alone can rescue him.' This is held up to ridicule, in order to attack even more vehemently the Christian apologetics that take the same line. The attack on the adulthood of the world is defined as 'pointless, ignoble and un-Christian'. This failure is ascribed by Bonhœffer to a misunderstanding of Christ. The central question for him concerns the relation of Christ to the newly matured world. Liberal theology failed because it allowed the world to assign Christ his place in the world. Bonhœffer was a true disciple of Harnack in his appreciation of the strength of liberal theology. Yet he saw that it failed—'in the dispute between Christ and the world it eventually accepted the comparatively clement peace dictated by the world.' But at least liberal theology saw that the battle had to be fought, even if it were lost to the superior forces of the world. This acceptance of the battle led to its overthrow. The church reacted with a return to the Bible and the Reformers. Bonhœffer shows the inadequacy of many of his contemporaries in their attempts to deal with the world come of age. Heim tried to convince modern man that he is faced with an alternative—despair or Jesus. Althaus reiterated Lutheranism and tried to gain a place in the world for Lutheran teaching and Lutheran worship. Tillich attempted to interpret the evolution of the world in a religious sense: 'the world unseated him and went on by itself: he too sought to understand the world better than it understood itself, but it felt entirely *mis*understood and rejected the imputation.' All these, says Bonhœffer, were 'sailing in the channel of liberal theology'. Barth first realised this and called in the God of Jesus Christ against religion—the spirit against the flesh. This Bonhœffer believes to be the greatest of Barth's contributions. He finds it in the second edition of his *Commentary on the Romans*. In his *Dogmatics*, Barth showed the church how to make the distinction between 'religion' and Christ. But he too failed to enable the church to discover a non-religious interpretation for its theological concepts. This was his limitation. This failure mattered a great deal to Bonhœffer because Barth passed it on to the Confessing Church which, in its resistance to the German Christians and through that resistance also to Nazism, lapsed into a conservative restoration of the orthodoxy of the Reformation. Bultmann of course did see Barth's limitation, as clearly as Bonhœffer did. But he too comes under fire for misconstruing the problem in terms of liberal theology and hence going 'off into the typical liberal reduction process.' Commenting on Bultmann's demythologizing, Bonhœffer says, 'I am of the view that the full content, including the mythological concepts, must be maintained. The New Testament is not a mythological garbing of the universal truth; this mythology (resurrection and so on) is the thing itself—but the concepts must be interpreted in such a way as not to make religion a pre-condition of faith. Not until that is achieved will liberal theology be overcome and the question it raises be genuinely taken up and answered.' He adds a little later, 'The world's coming of age . . . is better understood than it understands itself, namely on the basis of the Gospel and in the light of Christ.' He does not answer his question whether this leaves room for the church or whether religion is gone for good. But clearly, in his most radical statements about 'religionless Christianity' he is most careful to preserve a clear christology. It is the structures of religion that must go, not the proper consideration of Christ.

Yet even in these lectures on christology, Bonhœffer is not prepared to find a category for Christ. His questions are not, 'How is it possible for Christ to be both man and God?' His question about Christ is never 'How?' but always 'Who?' He will not even have a disguised 'What?' or 'How?' in the form of a 'Who?' Every avenue of his thinking leads him to confront Christ and ask, 'Who art thou, Lord?' or to be confronted by Christ and hear his question, 'Who do you say that I am?'

The material translated in this book is the substance of a series of lectures given during the summer semester (May-

July) in 1933 at the University of Berlin. The original
manuscript has not survived and the only text we have is
what Eberhard Bethge could reconstruct from the notes of
his fellow students. More than once, in his letters, Bonhœffer shows his complete confidence in Bethge to interpret
his thinking. When he was not able to complete a book he
always took consolation from the thought that he had
talked it all out with Bethge and that he would fill in the
blanks! He has done so admirably here. But the last
section is missing because Bonhœffer never finished the
course. This section cannot be written up and that is a
pity because he tells us that it was to have dealt with 'The
Eternal Christ'. It could have been an important addition
to our understanding of Bonhœffer's thought.

The lectures thus reconstructed, with all their limitations,
give us a glimpse into the mind of Dietrich Bonhœffer as
he dealt with his most important theme in the year 1933.
The year is significant. Earlier that year, Adolf Hitler had
been named Chancellor of Germany, the church had had
its first taste of a National Bishop, and the issue between
the Confessing Church and the German Christians had
been defined. Most men knew that a struggle was about
to begin which would be for the soul of Germany. None
saw this more clearly than Bonhœffer, who entered the
struggle with reluctance. That summer, on the day of the
church election, which was to put the German Christians
into power and give Hitler the means whereby he could
control the church, Bonhœffer preached a sermon telling of
his reluctant decision to enter the struggle. His text was
the classical text for the understanding of the nature of the
church, Matthew 16, 13-18. After announcing his text,
he declared his reluctance: 'If it were left to us, we would
rather avoid the decisions which are now forced upon us;
if it were left to us, we would rather not allow ourselves to

be caught up in this church struggle; if it were left to us, we would rather not have to insist upon the rightness of our cause and we would so willingly avoid the terrible danger of exalting ourselves over others . . . And yet, thank God, it is not left to us.'[1] That church election and the sermon took place at the end of the summer semester in which Bonhœffer had given his lectures on christology. The events, in which he was so deeply involved, may explain why the series was never finished. This kind of interference with his academic work also explains why he was reluctant to enter the struggle. Bonhœffer knew that his theology was important and he also knew that involvement in political struggle, even church political struggle, would distract him from his work. It is important to recognise that Bonhœffer regarded himself principally as a theologian. This tension was with him when he delivered the lectures contained in this book.

During the previous year, his main concern had been with his two major interests—Christian Ethics, or 'Ethics' as he preferred to call it, and the church. Both themes required a clarification of his christology. He had already made it quite clear that he accepted no authority for the church except that of Christ 'living and present in it'. At a Youth Peace Conference that year in Czechoslovakia, he had made this clear: 'From Christ alone must we know what we should do. But not from him as the preaching prophet of the Sermon on the Mount, but from him as the one who gives us life and forgiveness, as the one who has fulfilled the commandments of God in our place, as the one who brings and promises the new world . . . Thus we are completely directed towards Christ.'[2] This talk to the Youth Conference and the paper written a little earlier on 'What is the Church?' were both influenced by lectures he

[1] *No Rusty Swords*, p. 213.   [2] *No Rusty Swords*, p. 166.

gave in 1932 on 'The Nature of the Church'. These lectures compelled him to face the Ecumenical Movement with the need for a theological basis. That was why the talk in Czechoslovakia from which I have just quoted is called, 'A Theological Basis for the World Alliance'. All this intellectual activity was demanding a clear christology and the lectures in this book were prepared as much for Bonhœffer's own use as for that of his students.

One further influence before we turn to the lectures themselves. In the autumn of 1932, Bonhœffer worked over his lectures on the early chapters of Genesis, which were later published as *Schöpfung und Fall*.[1] The lectures add very little to the understanding of Genesis 1-3, which they set out to expound, but they nevertheless caused a stir among the students. They posed for Bonhœffer and his students the question of the place of Christ in creation and the relation of the work of Christ to the fall of man in the setting of a fallen world. Having raised this problem, he was committed to a series of lectures on christology, whether he wanted to or not. The Genesis lectures had already shown the influence of events on Bonhœffer's thinking. Events themselves were now demanding a clear statement on christology. The church struggle in Germany would require a theological basis as much as the World Alliance did, and that would later depend very much upon Bonhœffer. The statement when it came was called the Barmen Declaration, and it could not have been written without the earnest thought that Bonhœffer was now giving to christology.

This is one of the things that gives importance to these lectures. They stand between the developing theologian, influenced by all that he had read and thought on the great doctrinal issues, and the leader of the resistance, who was

[1] E.T. *Creation and Fall*, SCM Press, 1955.

determined that this resistance would be theological rather than political. Here, in this christological material, we have an arsenal from which the Confessing Church would draw many of its weapons to defeat the German Christians and thus prevent the poison of Nazism from destroying the church. That is why the material has a polemical note.

And now to the lectures themselves. They were divided into three parts, of which only the first two were delivered: the first part dealt with the Christ ever present in the Word, the Sacrament and the Church; the second part dealt with the Christ of history. One day a bold theologian will write the third part, on the Eternal Christ. Perhaps this is a task for Eberhard Bethge when the Biography is finished.

Bonhœffer refused to begin his lectures on christology with what he called the 'alchemy of the incarnation'. The classical discussion of the two natures seemed to him impertinent and certainly concerned with the wrong questions. The discussion which set out to ask 'What?' had been led into asking 'How?' and that was no question for man. Equally, he saw how the evasion of christology in the preaching of the cross led to a concentration upon the works of Christ to the exclusion of the real questions. The theologian must be able to speak of Jesus Christ as one in whom 'Act' and 'Being' are one. He is not required to answer the question 'How?', but is required to look seriously at the questions 'What?' and 'Where?' These, Bonhœffer proceeds to deal with.

What is Jesus Christ? leads to three answers—'Word', 'Sacrament' and 'Church'. The development of this can be read in the lectures. The strongest part of it is his discussion of the meaning of the Word. But those who have formed an opinion of Bonhœffer's thought from his last letters, particularly on the church, should pay careful attention to his 'high' doctrine of the church and the sacrament.

Where is Jesus Christ? leads to an examination of the self. Bonhœffer turns to the Reformers for his understanding of Christ as 'for me'. The locus of Christ is therefore found 'standing in my stead' and at the border of my existence. It is because I am separate from my true being that Christ thus stands between me as I am and me as I should be. He stands to judge and thereby to 'rediscover the authentic censure of my true being.' This is not the idealist's attempt to describe Christ as the centre of my being, which really means that the human personality is the highest expression of man and his point of contact with God. One does not therefore reason from human experience to Christ, but the other way. Christ interprets our being. We discover our humanity in him. He judges us from the border of our existence and he brings us new life. This argument can be traced carefully in these lectures and it remains permanent in Bonhœffer's thinking. Without this, he could not write his *Ethics*, and only by understanding this insight can we properly follow the argument in his last letters. Here, and especially in the first part, we have the basis for an understanding of such phrases as 'the man for others', 'man come of age'. These lectures are also necessary if we are to correct the false impression of Bonhœffer as the apostle of the 'dying church' or as the advocate of 'religionless Christianity' or 'worldly holiness'. The paradox of the catchphrases can only be resolved by the study of his christology. Only thus can Bonhœffer guide the post-war church as he knew he would.

When Bonhœffer made his fateful decision in July 1939 to return to Germany, he wrote to Reinhold Niebuhr, 'I will have no right to participate in the reconstruction of Christian life in Germany after the war if I do not share the trials of this time with my people.'[1] One of the assumptions he made was that he would be needed after the war in Germany. He was right. But had he remained in America, we might have had him now to co-operate in the rebuilding of the spiritual life in Germany and Europe. He would certainly have completed his lectures on christology. By returning, he did more. He was able to remain in touch with the different pressures up to the time of his death, and he comes to us through his writings, not as a pre-war theologian, but as one who lived it through. His last writings are sealed with his blood and are his legacy to a post-war Europe. The effect they are now having on our theological development even in Britain indicate how right his decision was.

Our principal danger today is that we shall only use those writings that came out of the experience of his last days. This would be an injustice to one of the greatest theologians of our time. The lectures in this book are necessary as a basis for understanding what Bonhœffer was hinting at in the occasional papers from prison. We need both the early framework of his thinking and the brilliant insights that he himself attempts to interpret within this framework. The two together give us the voice of the prophet.

Bonhœffer gave three answers to the question, 'Where is Jesus Christ today?' These three answers must be studied in the light of all he said later, because he never abandoned them.

1. Jesus Christ is at the border of *my* existence. With that word 'my' he ended the cold discussion of the nature of Christ as an academic exercise. The question has an answer *for me*, not for the textbook. At the border of my existence, he gives meaning to my existence and he gives the only meaning that makes sense and offers hope.

[1] *Gesammelte Schriften*, I, p. 320.

2. Jesus Christ is the centre and meaning of history. With this answer he rescued his theology from a purely personal experience. His christology is biblical and as such rooted in history. This is more than the true historicity of the man Jesus. This is not just 'the Jesus of history'. Again, Christ is not interpreted from history any more than he is interpreted from my experience. History is interpreted from him, as I am interpreted from him. This alone gives meaning to history and hope. At this point, Bonhœffer is nearest to Teilhard de Chardin.

3. Jesus Christ is the heart of nature. Bonhœffer does not deduce from nature that God is at work. He denies that it is possible to deduce God from nature. But he claims that Christ, who is already known, can be recognized in nature. He alone gives meaning to nature and hope. Here, Bonhœffer is closest to Paul.

These three answers force us away from the classical statement of christology. The Chalcedonian Definition is cold, statue cold, and requires the warm breath of life before it can be recognized as anything to do with Jesus Christ. Bonhœffer would have us discover the ever-present Christ in our existence, in the purpose of history and in the meaning of creation. Or rather all three are discovered to be meaningful in him.

Christ the Center

Introduction

I. THE CHRISTOLOGICAL QUESTION

Teaching about Christ begins in silence. 'Be silent, for that is the absolute' (Kierkegaard). This has nothing to do with mystical silence which, in its absence of words, is, nevertheless, the soul secretly chattering away to itself. The church's silence is silence before the Word. In proclaiming the Word, the church must fall silent before the inexpressible: Let what cannot be spoken be worshipped in silence (Cyril of Alexandria). The spoken Word is the inexpressible: that which cannot be spoken is the Word. It must be spoken, it is the great battle cry of the church (Luther). The church utters it in the world, yet it still remains the inexpressible. To speak of Christ means to keep silent; to be silent about Christ means to speak. The proclamation of Christ is the church speaking from a proper silence.

We are concerned here with the meaning of this proclamation. Its content is revealed only in the proclamation itself. To speak of Christ, then, will be to speak within the context of the silence of the church. We must study christology in the humble silence of the worshipping community. Prayer is to be silent and to cry out at the same time, before God in the presence of his Word. We have come together as a community to study Christ, God's Word. We have not met in church, but in the lecture room. We have academic work to do.

Christology is a peculiar discipline, because its subject is

Christ himself, the Word, the Logos. Christology is the science of the Word of God. Christology is *logology*. Christology is *the* science, because it is concerned with the Logos. Were this Logos our own Logos, then christology would be a matter of the Logos reflecting upon itself. But this Logos is the Logos of God, whose transcendence makes christology the crown of learning and whose coming from outside makes it the centre of scholarship. The subject remains transcendent and yet the Logos with whom we are concerned here is a person. This man is transcendent.

That means two things:

1. The Logos is not only an idea. Where the idea is thought of as the final reality of the Logos there can ultimately be no understanding of the central character of christology or of its pre-eminent place.

2. Because of its claim to be *the* discipline *par excellence* and the centre of its sphere, christology stands alone. There is no proof by which it can demonstrate the transcendence of its subject. Its statement that this transcendence, namely the Logos, is a person, a man, is a presupposition and not subject to proof. A transcendence which is allowed to be subject to proof instead of being the presupposition of thought is simply reason coming to an understanding of itself. Only a discipline which knows itself to be within the sphere of the church will be able to agree here that christology is the centre of the academic world. For the rest, it remains the unknown and hidden centre of the *universitas litterarum.*

All scientific questions can be reduced to two: *a.* What is the cause of *x*? *b.* What is the meaning of *x*? The first question embraces the sphere of the natural sciences, the second that of the arts. Both belong together. The subject *x* is comprehended by the natural sciences once it has been understood in its causal connection with other subjects.

INTRODUCTION

The subject *x* is comprehended by the arts once an understanding has been reached of its significance in relation to other known subjects. In both instances it is a matter of classification. An unknown subject becomes known through the possibility of finding a place for it in the already existing pattern. How does the subject *x* fit into the order which is already there? The question is directed towards the potentialities of the subject, towards its 'How?' The subject is defined, grasped, known by this 'How?' In other words, man's immanent Logos answers the question 'How?' posed by the need for classification. That is important in the case of christology. How can this subject be classified?

Man's ultimate presupposition lies in his human Logos, which engages in this process of classification. What happens if doubt is cast on this presupposition of his scientific activity? What if somewhere the claim is raised that this human Logos is superseded, judged, dead? What happens if an Anti-Logos appears which refuses to be classified? A Logos which annihilates the first? What if the proclamation goes out that the old order has been dissolved, that it is out of date, and that the counterpart of a new world has already begun? What answer does man's Logos give when it is addressed like this?

First of all, the human Logos repeats its old question. How is such a claim possible? How can such a claim be understood within its own order? It thus keeps on with its question, 'How?' But under this threat to its dominion from outside it now surpasses itself. It forestalls the claim by negating itself and at the same time asserting that this negation is a necessary development of its own being. This is the ultimate deceit and the ultimate power of this Logos. This is what Hegel did in his philosophy. This reaction of the Logos under the attack of the Anti-Logos is no narrow-minded repudiation of the other Logos, as in the Enlightenment, but the great insight into its power of self-negation. Self-negation, however, means self-affirmation. By limiting itself, the Logos reinstates itself in power. Nevertheless, the Logos recognizes the claim of the Anti-Logos. Thus the attempt to attack its ultimate presupposition seems to have failed. The Logos has assimilated the Anti-Logos into itself.

But what if the Anti-Logos raises his claim in a completely new form? If he is no longer an idea, but a Word, which challenges the supremacy of the Logos? If he appears at some time and in some place in history as a person? If he declares himself to be a judgment on the human Logos and points to himself: I am the Way, the Truth and the Life; I am the death of the human Logos, I am the life of God's Logos; man with his Logos must die, he falls into my hands; I am the first and the last?

If the Anti-Logos no longer appears in history as an idea, but as the Word incarnate, there is no longer any possibility of incorporating him into the order of man's own Logos. There is in fact only one question left: 'Who are you? Speak!' The question 'Who are you?' is the question of deposed, distraught reason. But it is equally the question of faith: Who are you? Are you God himself? This is the question with which christology is concerned. Christ is the Anti-Logos. There is no longer any possibility of classification because the existence of this Logos means the end of the human Logos. The question 'Who are you?' is the only appropriate question. To this question the phenomenon discloses itself. Christ gives an answer to the question 'Who?'

The question 'Who?' is the question of transcendence. The question 'How?' is the question of immanence. Because the one who is questioned here is the Son, the immanent question cannot grasp him. Not, 'How are you possible?'

—that is the godless question, the serpent's question—but 'Who are you?' The question 'Who?' expresses the strangeness and otherness of the encounter and at the same time reveals itself as the question of the very existence of the enquirer himself. He enquires about the being which is alien to his own being, about the boundaries of his own existence. Transcendence puts his own being in question. With the answer that his Logos has found its limit man comes up against the boundaries of his existence. So the question of transcendence is the question of existence and the question of existence is the question of transcendence. In theological terms: man only knows who he is in the light of God.

The question 'Who are you?' occurs in daily life. But, put loosely, it can sometimes be reduced to the question 'How?', the question of classification. Tell me how you are, tell me how you think, and I will tell you who you are. This secularised question 'Who?' is a remnant of the original religious question which any life poses. The question 'Who?' is *the* religious question. It is the question about the other man and his claim, about the other being, the other authority. It is the question about love for one's neighbour. The questions of transcendence and existence become a personal question. That means that man cannot answer the question 'Who?' by himself. Existence cannot emerge from itself; it remains relative to itself and merely mirrors itself in itself. Fettered in its own authority, it still goes on asking the question 'How?' The human heart is the *cor curvum in se* (Luther). If we ask, 'Who are you?', we may be *speaking* in the language of the obedient Adam, but we are *thinking* in the language of the fallen Adam; we are thinking, 'How are you?' This was the ruin of the first speech.

Can we put the strict question 'Who?' at all? In asking

'Who?', can we mean anything but 'How?'? We cannot. The mystery of this 'Who?' remains hidden. The ultimate question of critical thought is involved in the dilemma of having to ask 'Who?' and yet not being able to.

This means in the first place that the question must have been already answered before it was put correctly. The question 'Who?' can only legitimately be put where the person questioned has previously revealed himself and has eradicated the immanent Logos. The question 'Who?' presupposes an answer that has already been given.

This means in turn that the christological question can be put scientifically only in the context of the church. It can only be put where the basic presupposition, Christ's claim to be the Logos of God, has been accepted. It can only be put where God is sought because men already know him. There is no general blind seeking after God. Here a man can only seek what has already been found. 'You would not seek me had you not already found me' (Pascal). This idea also occurs in Augustine. Here, then, is the place at which christology must begin. In the church, in which Christ has revealed himself as the Word of God, the human Logos puts the question: Who are you, Jesus Christ, Word of God, Logos of God? The answer is given, the church receives it new every day. The human Logos seeks to understand it, to ponder it, to explain it.

Two questions are thus excluded from christological thought:

1. The question whether the answer which has already been given and the corresponding question 'Who?' from the church are justified or not. This question is quite illegitimate because there can be no reason for the human Logos to doubt the truth of the divine Logos. Jesus' testimony to himself stands by itself, self-authenticating. It is the backbone of any theology. The fact of the revelation

of God in Christ cannot be either established or disputed scientifically.

2. The question of how the 'fact' of the revelation can be conceived. This question is tantamount to going behind Christ's claim and providing an independent vindication of it. Here the human Logos presumes to be the beginning and the Father of Jesus Christ. With this inordinate claim the human Logos pretends to trinitarian form.

If these two questions are excluded there remains the question 'Who?', the question of the being, the essence and the nature of Christ. That means that the christological question is fundamentally an ontological question. Its aim is to work out the ontological structure of the 'Who?' without coming to grief on the Scylla of the question 'How?' or the Charybdis of the question of the 'fact' of revelation. The ancient church foundered on the former, modern theology since the Enlightenment and Schleiermacher has foundered on the latter. The New Testament, Paul and Luther have taken the middle course.

Let us return to the beginning. To what extent is the christological question the central question of scholarship? It has this significance inasmuch as it alone has put the question of transcendence in the form of the question of existence, inasmuch as the ontological question has here been put as the question of the being of a person, the person Jesus Christ. The old Logos is judged by the transcendence of the person of Christ and learns to understand it correctly within its necessary limitations. As logology, christology alone makes scholarship possible. But this is to touch only on the formal side.

The matter of content is more important. Human reason is strained to the limit by the question 'Who?' What happens when the Anti-Logos raises his claim? Man annihilates the 'Who?' with whom he is confronted. 'Who are you?' asks Pilate. Jesus is silent. Man cannot wait for the dangerous answer. The Logos cannot endure the Anti-Logos. It knows that one of them must die. So it kills the person of whom it has asked. Because the human Logos does not want to die, the Logos of God, who would be the death of it, must die so that it can live on with its unanswered questions of existence and transcendence. The Logos of God incarnate must be crucified by man's Logos. The one who compelled the dangerous question is killed, the question dies with him.

But what happens if this Counter-Word, though killed, rises living and victorious from the dead as the ultimate Word of God? If he sets himself up before his murderers? If the Crucified shows himself as the Risen One? Here the question 'Who are you?' reaches its sharpest climax. Here it stands vividly for ever over, around and in man, as question and as answer. Man can struggle against the Incarnate, but in the face of the Risen One he is powerless. Now he is himself the one who is judged and killed. The question is reversed and rebounds on the human Logos. 'Who are you, to ask thus?' 'Are you truly there, to ask thus?' 'Who are you, who can still only inquire after me when I restore you, justify you and give you my grace?'

The christological question 'Who?' is finally formulated only where this reversed question is also heard. The mere fact that man for his part can be questioned like this shows who it is who asks. Only God can ask like this. A man cannot put these questions to his fellow. In that case, the only question which can be returned is 'Who are you?' Questions of 'fact', the question 'How?' have lost all meaning.

What can that mean in particular? Even today the Unknown One meets men on the road in such a way that they can only ask the question 'Who are you?', however

often they try to parry it. They must come to grips with
him. We must also come to grips with Goethe and Socrates.
On this our education and our ethos depend. But on our
coming to grips with Christ depend life and death, salvation
and damnation. This cannot be appreciated from outside.
But in the church it is the principle on which everything
rests. 'And there is salvation in no one else' (Acts 4.12).
The cause of the encounter with Jesus is not the same as
that of the encounter with Socrates and Goethe. It is
impossible to avoid the person of Jesus because he is alive.
If need be, Goethe can be avoided because he is dead.
Thousands of attempts have been made to resist or to avoid
meeting Jesus.

For the working-class world, Christ seems to be settled
with the church and bourgeois society. There is no longer
any reason why the worker should encounter Jesus Christ.
The church is all one with the fossilised sanctions of the
capitalist system. But at this very point, the working class
may distinguish between Jesus and his church; *he* is not
the guilty party. Up with Jesus, down with the church.
Here Jesus can become the idealist, the socialist. What does
it mean when, in his world of suspicion and distrust, the
worker says, 'Jesus was a good man'? It means that there
is no need to distrust *him*. The worker does not say 'Jesus
is God.' But when he says 'Jesus was a good man' he is at
any rate saying more than when the bourgeois says, 'Jesus
is God.' God for him is something which belongs to the
church. But Jesus can be present on the factory floor as the
socialist, in politics as the idealist, in the workers' own world
as the good man. He fights in their ranks against the enemy,
capitalism. Who are you? Are you our brother and Lord?
Is the question merely evaded here? Or do they, in their
own way, put it seriously?

Dostoievsky portrayed the figure of Christ in the splendour

of Russian culture in his novel, *The Idiot*. The idiot does not keep himself apart, but clumsily causes offence everywhere. He has nothing to do with the great ones, but with the children. He is mocked and he is loved. He is the fool and he is the wise man. He endures all and he forgives all. He is revolutionary, yet he conforms. He does not want to —but he draws attention to himself simply by being there. Who are you? Idiot or Christ?

One might think of Gerhard Hauptmann's novel, *Der Narr in Christo Emanuel Quint*; or of the descriptions and distortions of Christ written by Wilhelm Gross and Georg Grosz, behind which there lurks the question, 'Who are you really?' Christ goes through the ages, questioned anew, missed anew, killed anew.

The theologian makes the same attempts to encounter Jesus or to get round him. Theologians betray him and simulate concern. Christ is always betrayed by the kiss. To want to deal with him always means to fall prostrate with the mockers and to say, 'Hail, Rabbi!' In the end, there are only two possibilities of encountering Jesus: either man must die or he kills Jesus.

The question 'Who are you?' remains ambiguous. It can be the question of the one who knows that he has been encountered and can hear already the counter-question, 'And who are you?' But it can also be the question of the person who, when he asks, means, 'How can I deal with you?' In that case, the question is simply a disguised form of the question 'How?' The question 'Who?' can be put to Jesus only when the counter-question has been heard. In that case it is not man who has dealt with Jesus, but Jesus who has dealt with man. So the question 'Who?' is to be spoken only in faith.

As long as the christological question is the question of the human Logos, it remains stuck in the ambivalence of the question 'How?' But if it is asked in the act of faith, it has the possibility of putting the question 'Who?'

There are two contrasting types of authority: the authority of the office and the authority of the person. The question to the authority of the office is, 'What are you?' The 'What?' concerns the office. The question to the authority of the person is, 'Whence do you have this authority?' The answer is, 'From you, who acknowledge my authority over you.' Both questions can be derived from the question 'How?' and can be assigned a place within it. It assumes that basically, each man is as I am. The presupposition is that the person who is asked can be similar to me in his being. The authorities are merely bearers of the authority of a community, bearers of an office, bearers of a word. They are not the office itself or the word itself. Even the prophets are what they are only as bearers of a word. But what happens if someone appears with the claim that he not only *has* authority but *is* authority; not only *has* a word but *is* the Word? Here our being is invaded by a new being. Here the highest authority in the world so far, the prophet, is at an end. This is no longer a holy man, a reformer, a prophet, but the Son. The question is no longer, 'What or whence are you?' The question here concerns revelation itself.

II. THE PERSON AND WORK OF CHRIST

Christology is not soteriology. What is the relationship between the two? How is the doctrine of the person of Christ related to the doctrine of the work of Christ? The classic statement in Melancthon's *Loci* runs: *Hoc est Christum cognoscere, beneficia eius cognoscere; non quod isti* (i.e. the Scholastics) *docent; eius naturas modos incarnationis contueri.* Here the christological question is derived from the soteriological question and settled in it. Who Christ is, is known here only from his works. As a result, a specific christology must be regarded as superfluous. This was an epoch-making view. It was carried on by Schleiermacher and Ritschl.

Put systematically, the question runs: Does the work interpret the person or the person the work? Luther often repeats that everything depends on whether the person is good; if the person is good, the work is also good, even if it does not seem to be so. On the other hand, if the work is good, it is impossible to make inferences from that about the person. The work may seem to be good, but it can still be the work of the devil. The devil appears in the form of an angel of light. The work may seem evil, but it can still be God's work. Any other view of man leads to justification by works. For Luther, the person interprets the work.

The person, however, cannot be known by us, but only by God. 'The Lord knows his own' (2 Tim. 2.19). So there is no access to the work except through the person; and access to the person is barred to us by the mystery of God's predestination. Any attempt nevertheless to grasp the person by the work remains unsuccessful because the work is ambivalent. There is no access to man unless he reveals himself of his own accord. This happens effectively in the church in the forgiveness of sins. Here one man presents himself to another as a sinner, confesses and has his sins forgiven by his brother. In the church it is thus possible to know another's person.

These thoughts are analogous to the situation in christology. I have access to the work of Christ only if I know the person who does this work. It is essential to know the person if the work is also to be known. If Jesus was the idealistic founder of a religion, I can be elevated by his work and stimulated to follow his example. But my sins are not forgiven, God still remains angry and I remain in the power of death. Jesus' work leads to despair in myself, because I cannot imitate his pattern. But if Jesus is the Christ, the Word of God, then I am not primarily called to emulate him; I am encountered in his work as one who could not possibly do this work myself. Through his work I recognize the gracious God. My sins are forgiven, I am no longer in death but in life. Whether his work perishes in the world of death or whether it abides in a new world of life depends upon the person of Christ. But how is the person of Christ to be recognized otherwise than through his work, i.e. otherwise than through history? This objection contains a most profound error. For even Christ's work is not unequivocal. It remains open to the most ambiguous interpretations. His work also allows the interpretation that he is a hero; his cross, the interpretation that it was the consummate act of a brave man remaining true to his convictions. There is no point in the life of Jesus to which one could point and say clearly, 'Jesus here was indubitably the Son of God,' 'Jesus here can clearly be recognized from one of his works.' No, he did his work in the incognito of history, in the flesh. The incognito of the incarnation makes it doubly impossible to recognize the person from his works:

1. Jesus is man and it is an ambiguous procedure to infer the person from the work.

2. Jesus is God and it is impossible to argue directly from history to God.

If this way of knowledge is excluded, there remains just one more attempt possible to gain access to Jesus Christ. This is the attempt to be in the place where the person reveals himself in his own being, without any compulsion. That is the place of prayer to Christ. Only through the word of free self-revelation is the person of Christ, and thus his work, disclosed.

In this way the theological priority of the christological question over the soteriological question has been demonstrated. If I know *who* the person is who does this I will also know *what* he does. But it would be false to conclude from this that person and work could be separated from each other. We are concerned here with the connection between person and work in knowledge, not in reality. The separation of the question of christology from that of soteriology is in fact necessary only for theological method. For the christological question, of its very nature, must be addressed to the whole Christ, the one Christ. This whole Christ is the historical *(geschichtliche)*[1] Jesus who can never in any way be divorced from his work. He is asked and he replies as the one who is himself his work. But christology primarily seeks his being and not his action. To put it in abstract terms: the subject of christology is the personal structure of being of the whole, historical Jesus Christ.

---

[1] Bonhœffer does not seem to distinguish the two German adjectives for ' historical '—*historisch* and *geschichtlich*—as precisely as some other German theologians, e.g. Bultmann. Sometimes, particularly on pp. 71 ff., he even uses them interchangeably. No attempt, therefore, has been made to find two distinctive English renderings. Where there is any possibility of confusion, the German has been added in brackets. (Tr.)

The Present Christ —
The 'Pro Me'

The Present Christ—the 'Pro Me'

Jesus is the Christ present as the Crucified and Risen One. That is the first statement of christology. 'Present' is to be understood in a temporal and spatial sense, *hic et nunc*. So it is part of the definition of the person. Both come together in the concept of the church.

Christ is present in the church as a person. That is the second christological definition. Only because Christ is present can we enquire of him. This presence is the presupposition for the development of the christological question. Only because preaching and sacrament take place in the church can Christ be sought after. The understanding of his presence opens the way for the understanding of the person.

This understanding is open to two severe misinterpretations:

a. The presence of Christ can be understood as the influence which emanates from him, which extends into the community. It is not Christ himself who is present, but his effective historical influence. Christ is conceived of here essentially in dynamic terms, not dissipating his energy in a series of historical events, but progressing through history. The presence of Christ is here conceived of in terms of cause and effect. He is present and therefore his influence must be felt.

b. Attempts are continually made to elucidate a picture of Christ which is outside history, whether it is the idealistic picture drawn by those of the Enlightenment or the spiritual picture of the inner life of Jesus drawn by such men as Wilhelm Herrmann.

Both misinterpretations often go hand in hand, as in Schleiermacher. Ritschl represents the first, his pupil Herrmann the second. Common to both is a christological error. Christ is understood from his historical influence, he is essentially power, *dynamis*, and not personal. This *dynamis* can be envisaged in different ways; as the echo of historical activity or as the newly emerging picture of the ideal character of the man Jesus. Here the historical force corresponds more with the temporal, the *nunc*, and the ideal power more with the spatial, the *hic*; the former thinks in the category of the cause, the latter in the category of the idea.

Here Christ is essentially conceived of not as a person, but as a power. This is even true where the 'personality' of Jesus is spoken of. In this context 'personality' means the opposite of what is meant by person. 'Personality' is the fullness and harmony of the values which are combined in the phenomenon Jesus Christ. 'Personality' is fundamentally an apersonal concept. It ends up in the neuters 'power' and 'value'. But in that case the christological question is obliterated. Person, on the other hand, goes beyond 'activity' and 'image', 'power' and 'value'. The questions which are put about personality are 'How?' and 'What?'; about the person, the question is 'Who?' Jesus as personality, power, value, exhausts his being in his work; his person, in his action. In that case the only possible thing is to infer the person from the work.

Hidden in the background of this idea of Christ there lies the fact that it does not deal with the resurrection, but only with Jesus up to the cross, with the historical Jesus. This is the dead Christ, who can be thought of like Socrates and

Goethe. Only the Risen One makes possible the presence of the living person and gives the presupposition for christology, no longer dissipated into historical energy or an intuited ideal of Christ.

Luther attempted to interpret the presence of Christ in the light of the ascension. Christ can be the one who is present by virtue of the fact that he sits at the right hand of God. 'When he was on earth he was far from us. Now he is far from us, he is near to us.' That means that only the Risen One, who has ascended to heaven, can be present with us, and not the one who is only within history. Ritschl and Herrmann put the resurrection on one side, Schleiermacher symbolizes it; in so doing they destroy the church. Paul says: 'If Christ has not been raised, your faith is futile and you are still in your sins' (1 Cor. 15.17).

Here we are confronted with the first problem of christology: if Christ is present not only as power, but in his person, how are we to conceive of this presence so that it does not violate the wholeness of his person? To be present means to be in the same place at the same time. Even as the Risen One, Jesus Christ remains the man Jesus in space and time. Only because Jesus Christ is man is he present in time and place. Only because Jesus Christ is God is he eternally present everywhere. The presence of Christ necessitates the statement 'Jesus is fully man'—and it necessitates the other statement, 'Jesus is fully God.' The contemporaneity and presence of Jesus Christ in the church are predicates of the one whole person, of the God-man. The question how the man Jesus, restricted by space and time, can be contemporaneous with us, is therefore impossible. This Jesus does not exist in isolation. The other question, how God can be in time, is equally impossible. This isolated God does not exist. The only possible meaningful question is, 'Who is present and contemporaneous with us here?'

The answer is, 'The one person of the God-man Jesus Christ.' I do not know who this man Jesus Christ is unless I say at the same time 'Jesus Christ is God', and I do not know who the God Jesus Christ is unless I say at the same time 'Jesus Christ is man.' The two factors cannot be isolated because they are not isolated. God in timeless eternity is not God, Jesus limited by time is not Jesus. Rather, God is God in the man Jesus. In this Jesus Christ God is present. This one God-man is the starting point of christology.

Space and time determine not only the humanity, but also the Godhead of the God-man. This one who is present in space and time, the God-man, is concealed in the likeness of human flesh, i.e. in the likeness of man (Rom. 8.3). The presence is a concealed presence. But it is not as though God were concealed in the man; rather, this God-man as a whole is concealed in this world in the likeness of man. In other words, the principle of concealment is not the man as such, not space and time, but the likeness of man, i.e. the world between temptation and sin.

In this way the whole problem of christology is shifted. For here the point at issue is not the relationship of an isolated God to an isolated man in Christ, but the relationship of the already given God-man to the likeness of man. This God-man Jesus Christ is present and contemporaneous in the form of the 'likeness', i.e. in veiled form, as a stumbling block (*scandalon*). This is the central problem of christology.

The presence of the already given God-man Jesus is concealed for us, and exists in the *scandalon* form of proclamation —a stumbling block to the Jews (1 Cor. 1.23). The proclaimed Christ is the real Christ. This proclamation is not a second incarnation. The offence caused by Jesus Christ is not his incarnation—that indeed is revelation—but his humiliation. The humanity of Christ and his humiliation should be carefully distinguished. Jesus Christ is man both as the Humiliated One and as the Exalted One. Only the humiliation is the stumbling block. The doctrine of the *scandalon* has its place not in the doctrine of the incarnation of God but in the doctrine of the state of humiliation of the God-man. The 'likeness of man' is part of the humiliation. Now that means for us that Christ is present as the Risen and Exalted One only in proclamation, and that means at the same time: only by way of a new humiliation. In proclamation the Risen and Exalted One is thus present in his humiliation. This presence has a threefold form in the church, that of the Word, the sacraments and the community.

But the basic question about Christ's presence has still not been answered. The question may not run: 'How can the man Jesus, or how can the God Christ be contemporaneous here?' There is no question about the fact of his presence. The question must run: 'By virtue of what personal structure is Christ present to the church?'

If we answer, 'By virtue of his being God and man', we may be correct, but that will be no explanation. The personal structure must be outlined more closely and developed as the *pro me* structure of the God-man Jesus Christ. Christ is Christ not as Christ in himself, but in his relation to me. His being Christ is his being *pro me*. This being *pro me* is in turn not meant to be understood as an effect which emanates from him, or as an accident; it is meant to be understood as the essence, as the being of the person himself. This personal nucleus itself is the *pro me*. That Christ is *pro me* is not an historical or an ontical statement, but an ontological one. That is, Christ can never be thought of in his being in himself, but only in his relationship to me. That in turn means that Christ can only be conceived of existentially, viz. in the community. Christ is not a Christ in himself and additionally still in the community. He who alone is the Christ is the one who is present in the community *pro me*. Luther says: 'So it is one thing if God is there, and another if he is there for you' (WA 23, 152). It is not only useless to meditate on a Christ in himself, but even godless. Hence we can understand Melancthon's defence in the *Loci*, which ends in a repudiation of any christology. A christology which does not put at the beginning the statement, 'God is only God *pro me*, Christ is only Christ *pro me*,' condemns itself. Then, of course, specifically christological work begins with this presupposition. Theology has often apostasized here. Either it has continued its scholastic beginnings and has volatilized the 'being for you' in an independent existence, or it has only considered the actions and the effects of Christ. But the decisive element in the *pro me* structure is that the being and action of Christ are maintained within it. *Actio Dei* and *præsentia Dei*, the being *for you* and the *being* for you, are combined. When the unity of act and being in Jesus Christ is understood in this way, the question of his person, i.e. the question 'Who?', can be rightly put. He is the one who has really bound himself to me in free existence. And he is the one who has freely preserved his contingency in his 'being-there for you'. He does not *have* the power of this being *pro me*, he *is* this power.

This *pro me* structure means three things for the relationship of Christ to the new humanity:

1. Jesus Christ *pro me* is pioneer, head and firstborn of the brethren who follow him. This *pro me* structure is thus related to the historicity of Jesus. He is *pro me* as pioneer for the others.

2. Jesus Christ is for his brethren by standing in their place. Christ stands for his new humanity before God. But if that is the case, he is the new humanity. He stands vicariously where mankind should stand, by virtue of his

pro me structure. He is the community. Not only does he act for it, he is it, by going to the cross, bearing sin, and dying. So mankind is crucified, dies, and is judged in him.

3. Because he acts as the new humanity, it is in him and he is in it. Because the new humanity is in him, God is gracious towards it in him.

This one, whole, person, the God-man Jesus Christ, is present in the church in his *pro me* structure as Word, as sacrament and as community.

To begin christology with this statement of one who is present, has the advantage that Jesus is understood from the start as the Risen One who has ascended into heaven. The difficulty then consists in maintaining the unity of act and being; either Christ is *there*, in which case he is not essentially *pro me* but even independent of me; or he is essentially there *for me*, and in that case is he also there apart from me?

I. THE FIGURE OF CHRIST

1. Christ as Word

1. Christ, the Word, is the truth. Truth is only in the Word and through the Word. Spirit is originally Word and language and not power, emotion and act. 'In the beginning was the Word . . . all things were made through him' (John 1.1,3). Only as Word is the Spirit also power and action. God's Word creates and destroys. 'The Word of God is . . . sharper than any two-edged sword, piercing' (Heb. 4.12). God's Word is behind the destruction of lightning and the life-giving rain. As Word it destroys and creates the truth.

It is trivial and irrelevant to ask whether God could have revealed himself otherwise than through the Word. Of course God is free to reveal himself in other ways or to follow courses that we do not know of. But God has revealed himself in the Word. He has bound himself to the Word so as to speak it to men. He does not alter this Word.

2. Christ is Word and not colour, form or stone. Christ is there as Word for man's sake. Man is driven to understand the meaning of things. His existence differs from that of the animal by virtue of its meaningfulness. As man has a Logos, God encounters him in the Logos who speaks and is himself the Word. The *homo sapiens* speaks, and that makes him the *homo sapiens*. The word conveys unequivocal, clear meaning. Clarity and straightforwardness are part of its make up. It explains itself. Clarity and straightforwardness are the basis of its universal validity. Clarity and straightforwardness are part of the make-up of the Word of God. The divine Logos is truth and meaning.

In Christ, the divine Logos has entered the human Logos; that is the humiliation of Jesus Christ. It should, however, be noted here that the Logos of God may not be identified with the human Logos, as in German idealism, nor may it be thought of as analogous to it, as in Catholicism. For that would amount to self-redemption, and the human Logos would escape judgment by the Christ-Logos.

3. Christ as the Logos of God remains distinct and divorced from the human Logos. He is the Word in the form of living address to men, whereas the word of man is word in the form of the idea. Address and idea are the basic structures of the word. But both exclude each other. Human thought is dominated by the form of the word as idea. The idea rests in itself, and is relative to itself; it extends its validity over space and time. When Christ today is called the Word of God this usually happens as a result

of this understanding of the idea. An idea is universally accessible, it is already there. Man can appropriate it of his own free will. Christ as idea is timeless truth; the idea of God embodied in Jesus is accessible to any one at any time.

The word as address stands in contrast to this. Whereas the Word as idea can remain by itself; as address, it can only be between two persons. Address leads to answer and it is answerable. It is not timeless, but takes place in history. It does not rest, and it is not accessible to any one at any time. It happens only where the address is made. The word lies wholly at the disposal of the person who speaks. So it is always new. The nature of Word as address demands a community. The nature of the truth in this word of address makes it seek community to bring about an encounter in the truth. Truth is not something which rests in itself and for itself, but something which takes place between two persons. Truth happens only in community. Only here does the concept of the Word acquire its full significance.

Christ as Word in the sense of address is thus not timeless truth. He is truth spoken in the concrete moment, the address which puts a man in the truth before God. He is not a universally accessible idea, but the Word perceived only where he allows himself to be perceived. Not flesh and blood, but the Father in heaven (Matt. 16.17) reveals the Christ where and when he will.

Christ as Word in the sense of address is only then properly the Christ *pro me*. So this definition of Christ as the word of address gives appropriate expression both to the contingency of revelation and to its connection with men.

4. In the light of these presuppositions, the content of the word of address is also defined. Its content is not the unveiling of hidden truths, the recounting of a new concept of God or a new moral doctrine. It is much more a case of

the personal address of God in which he calls men to answer for themselves. In his being as he is and his being there, man is put in the truth. Christ becomes the address of forgiveness and of command. It does not matter whether the command is old or new—it can be either old or new—all that matters is that it happens. Similarly, that forgiveness happens. Command and forgiveness take place, however, because the Word of God is the person of Christ.

5. The relationship between word and person can be thought of in different ways. The person of Christ can be thought of as the bearer of an idea; he can be thought of as a prophet; through him God speaks. He *says* the word without *being* the Word. In that case the important thing would not be his person, but his mission. But the New Testament contradicts this understanding. There Christ points to himself: 'I *am* the way, the truth and the life' (John 14.6). And this is attested as *the* sole possibility of God's revelation, happening in the one who does not *have* the Word in his person, but *is* the Word. He is the Word as the Son.

6. Christ is not only present *in* the word of the church but also *as* the word of the church, i.e. as the spoken word of preaching. '*In* the word' might say too little, if it made it possible to separate Christ from his Word. Christ's presence is his existence as preaching. The whole Christ is present in preaching, Christ humiliated and Christ exalted. His presence is not that power of the community or its objective spirit from which the preaching is made, but his existence as preaching. Were that not so, preaching could not have the prominent place accorded to it by the Reformation. This place belongs to even the simplest preaching. Preaching is the riches and the poverty of the church. It is the form of the presence of Christ to which we are bound and to which we have to keep. If the whole

Christ is not in the preaching then the church breaks in pieces. The relationship between God's Word and man's word in preaching is not that of exclusiveness. The human word of preaching is not a phantom body for the Word of God. But the Word of God has really entered into the humiliation of the word of man. Man's word of preaching is the Word of God by virtue of God's voluntary association, by which he has bound himself to the word of man. Luther remarked, 'You shall point to this man and say, "That is God." ' To alter it slightly, 'You shall point to this word of man and say, "That is the Word of God." ' Both sentences are ultimately identical. One cannot point to this word of man without pointing to this man Jesus, who is God.

So Christ is present in the church as the spoken Word, not as music and not as art. He is present as the spoken Word of judgment and forgiveness. Two things must be said here with equal emphasis: 'I could not preach if I did not know that I were speaking the *Word of God*'; and: 'I could not preach did I not know that *I* were not speaking the Word of God.' Human impossibility and God's promise are one and the same.

2. Christ as Sacrament

Two things are to be said here: Christ is wholly Word and yet the sacrament, too, fully mediates the presence of the Word. In other words, the sacrament is distinct from the Word and has a specific justification for its existence.

1. The sacrament is the Word of God, for it is the proclamation of the Gospel. It is not a mystery or a mute symbolic action, but an action consecrated and interpreted through the Word. The promise of the forgiveness of sins

makes the sacrament what it is: clear revelation. Anyone who believes the Word in the sacrament has the whole sacrament.

2. The Word in the sacrament is an embodied Word. It is not a representation of the Word. Only something which is not present can be represented. But the Word is present. The elements of water, bread and wine, named by God by name, become sacraments. Through the address of the Word of God they become the corporeal form of the sacrament just as the creature only becomes creature when God addresses it by name. The word of preaching is the form in which the Logos reaches the human Logos. The sacrament is the form in which the Logos reaches man in his nature. If it is asserted here that the subject only becomes what it is by being given its name, we must notice a difference from philosophical conceptualism. The fallen creation is no longer the creation of the first creative Word. Man's 'I' is no longer what was named by God, people no longer people, history no longer history. The word is no longer seen in creation. The continuity of Word and nature has been lost. The creation is not a sacrament. There is only a sacrament where in the midst of the creaturely world God addresses, names and hallows an element with his special Word.

Thus the eucharist is what it is by God addressing and hallowing the elements of bread and wine with his Word. This Word is called Jesus Christ. Through Jesus Christ the sacrament is interpreted and hallowed. God has bound himself to the sacrament of these elements through this Word, Jesus Christ. This Word Jesus Christ is wholly present in the sacrament, not only his Godhead, and not only his manhood.

3. True, Jesus Christ is the Word spoken by God even in the sacrament. But against the attempt to limit Christ

to doctrine, to volatilize him in general truth, the church stresses the sacramental form of Christ. He is not only *doctrina*, or even idea, but nature and history. The insufficiencies of nature and history are God's cloak. But not everything corporeal, not all nature and history are meant to be sacramental. Nature as such does not symbolize Christ. His presence remains restricted to the forms of preaching and the two sacraments.

Why these particular sacraments? Protestant dogmatics says because they are actions instituted by Jesus. But this should not be understood as an expression of historicism. Institution by Jesus can only mean a gift from the exalted and present Christ to his community. The number of sacraments in which Christ is present cannot be substantiated otherwise than through reference to this institution by the exalted Lord, i.e. in this sense purely positivistically. Qualified in this way, they do not stand as a symbol for something else; they *are* the Word of God. They do not *mean* something, they *are* something.

4. The sacrament is not a concealment of the bodiless Word of God under the veil of a corporeal form, so that the sacrament could be considered as a second incarnation. The one who has been made flesh, made man, is in the sacrament in the form of a stumbling block. The sacrament is not an incarnation of God but an act of humiliation on the part of the God-man. This is analogous to what was said earlier, that christology is not primarily concerned with the question of the possibility of the union of God and man but rather with the concealment of the presence of the God-man in his humiliation. God is made manifest in the flesh, but concealed as an offence. It follows from this that the question of the presence of Christ in the sacrament may not be presented and analyzed as a question of the manhood and Godhead of Christ but merely as the question of

the presence of the God-man in the form of his humiliation or as a stumbling block.

5. A labyrinth of misunderstandings developed in Protestant theology because questions were put wrongly. The questions related on the one hand to the possibility of a presence of Christ in the sacrament, and on the other hand to the relationship between Christ's being *there* and being *pro me*.

In the words of institution at the Last Supper, Christ said that he would be present to the church as man. Luther would not allow this saying to be modified. He clung to the recognition that the man Jesus must be present if Christ's work is to benefit us. Everything depends on the contemporaneity and presence of the man Jesus Christ. So for Luther the whole Gospel hung on Jesus' words of institution.

This position was attacked when it was pointed out that Jesus Christ was nevertheless the one who has ascended to heaven. Reformed theologians asked how it could be possible that the one who sits at the right hand of God is present. First of all, Luther burst out in mocking laughter at the question: God must not be imagined to be in space like a bird in a nest (WA 23, 158). The Reformed theologians argued that Christ as the person of the Logos was extra-corporeal during the sacrament. The Logos was not involved in his corporeality, but remained outside. This *extra-Calvinisticum* is the result of the question 'How?' But Lutheran theology allowed the question to be posed. Luther answered the Reformed question with the doctrine of ubiquity. As the body of the God-man, the body of Jesus took divine properties in the *communicatio* with the divine nature. This body of Jesus is not limited in space, but is present in all places at the same time by virtue of the *genus maiestaticum*. The transfigured body is present everywhere;

so too, therefore, is Christ's humanity in the eucharist.
Luther knows three different modes of presence:

a. localiter or *circumscriptive*, just as the earthly body of
Jesus Christ was tangibly present (WA 26, 337);

b. diffinitive, like the angels and demons who are everywhere and yet in a particular place (WA 26, 328);

c. repletive, where something is everywhere and yet can
nowhere be measured and defined (WA 26, 329).

According to Luther, Jesus Christ is present in this third
mode, described under *c.*, everywhere and yet intangible.
He is not in the bread like straw in a sack; this *'in'* must
be understood theologically. He is only where he reveals
himself in his Word. 'It is solely a question of revelation.
He is everywhere, but you will not be able to grasp him
unless he offers himself to you, and himself interprets the
bread to you through the Word. You will not eat him
unless he wishes to reveal himself to you' (Luther WA 19,
492; 23, 151). Christ is even in the rustling leaf, as Luther
says, but he is not there *for you*, i.e. he is not manifest.

What is the christological significance of these statements?
Christology here has become eucharistic christology. Its
thought is governed by the eucharist. But Luther has
answered the question 'How?' Luther answered the question
'How is Christ present?' with two different doctrines, the
doctrine of ubiquity (Christ is present everywhere) and the
doctrine of ubivoluntarianism (Christ is only present for
you where he wills to be there for you). Both doctrines are
impossible metaphysical hypostatisations. In each an
element of reality is isolated and elevated into a system.
None of the expressions is appropriate to what it is meant
to describe. In so far as Christ is everywhere, the fact that
he is a person is overlooked. In so far as his presence, where
he wills, is *in actu*, this presence is not understood as a mode
of existence.

Christ's being there and his being for you must be given simultaneous attention. Ubiquitarianism teaches a Christ outside revelation; revelation becomes the accident of a substance which is at hand. Ubivoluntarianism teaches the presence of Christ not as a particular definition of the person but as a promise bound up with Jesus' Word. The two doctrines do not understand Christ's presence *pro me* as his mode of existence. They are theologically inadequate, as they cannot give appropriate expression to the presence of the God-man, the person of the Exalted and Humiliated One. They answer the question 'How?' and necessarily lead to a conceptual *impasse*. They were the result of questions put by the Reformed theologians to Luther, and they brought confusion to late Lutheran theology. Nevertheless, even the *impasse* is better and more to the point than the rationalistic simplification of Schleiermacher, who adapted the content of the facts to the question 'How?'

6. The question of Christ's presence in the sacrament cannot be answered in the light of the question 'How?' *Who* is present in the sacrament? This is the only form in which the question can be put. The answer runs: the whole person of the God-man is present in his exaltation and his humiliation; Christ exists in such a way that he is existentially present in the sacrament. His being sacramental is not a special property, one quality among others; this is the way he exists in the church. The humiliation is not the accident of his divine-human substance, but his existence.

Is there a Christ of the sacrament and a Christ of preaching? Is the one who is present in the sacrament different from the one who is present as the Word? No. He is the one Christ, who judges and who forgives, who is the Word both here and there. In the Word he makes use of our human Logos; in the sacrament he makes use of our body and is present in the sphere of tangible nature. In the sacrament Christ is beside us as creature, in our midst, brother with brother. But in being a creature he is also the new creature. In the sacrament he is the penetration of fallen creation at a particular point. He is the new creature. He is the restored creation of our spiritual and bodily existence.

He is the Word of God made bread and wine. As new creature he is in the bread and in the wine. So bread and wine are a new creation. They are real nourishment for the new being. As elements of the restored creation they are of course nothing for themselves, but for men. This being-for-men is what makes them a new creation.

The Christ present in the sacrament is the creator of this new creation and is at the same time a creature. He is present as our creator, who makes us new creatures. But he is also present as the humbled creature in the sacrament, and not otherwise. This is the way in which he is present.

The question *how* that can be must be changed into the question *who* this person is. The answer is, the historical (*geschichtliche*) Jesus who was crucified, who is risen and ascended to heaven, the God-man, revealed as brother and Lord, as creature and as creator.

3. Christ as Community

Just as Christ is present as the Word and in the Word, as the sacrament and in the sacrament, so too he is also present as community and in the community. His presence in Word and sacrament is related to his presence in the community as reality is to figure. Christ is the community by virtue of his being *pro me*. His form, indeed his only form, is the community between the ascension and the second coming. The fact that he is in heaven on the right hand of God does not contradict this; on the contrary, it alone makes possible his presence in and as the community.

What does it mean that Christ as *Word* is also community? It means that the Logos of God has extension in space and time in and as the community. Christ, the Word, is spiritually and physically present. The Logos is not only the weak word of human teaching, *doctrina*; he is also the powerful Word of creation. He speaks, and thus creates the form of the community. The community is therefore not only the receiver of the Word of revelation; it is itself revelation and Word of God. Only in so far as it is itself the Word of God can it understand the Word of God. Revelation can be understood only on the basis of revelation. The Word is *in* the community in so far as the community is a recipient of revelation. But the Word is also itself community in so far as the community is itself revelation and the Word wills to have the form of a created body.

What does it mean that Christ as *sacrament* is also community? Christ the sacrament is also there in and as the community. The sacrament already in itself has a physical form which goes beyond the Word. The community is the body of Christ. Body here is not just a metaphor. The community *is* the body of Christ, it does not *represent* the body of Christ. Applied to the community, the concept of the body is not just a functional concept which merely refers to the members of this body; it is a comprehensive and central concept of the mode of existence of the one who is present in his exaltation and his humiliation.

This Christ existing as community is the whole person, as the one who is exalted and humiliated. His being as community, like his being as Word and sacrament, has the form of a stumbling block. In so far as it is community, it is no longer in sin. But it remains in the world of the old Adam, in the likeness of man, under the era of sin. It remains human in repentance. (See 1 John.)

Christ is not only the head of the community but also the community itself. (Cf. 1 Cor. 12 and the Epistle to the Ephesians.) Christ is head and every member. Only in the Epistle to the Ephesians does the separation between head and members appear; it is not originally Pauline. The head means the Lordship. But the two expressions do not contradict one another.

II. THE PLACE OF CHRIST

If we look for the place of Christ, we are looking for the structure of the 'Where?' within that of the 'Who?' We are thus remaining within the structure of the person. Everything depends on Christ being present to his church as a person in space and time. If this structure can be demonstrated to be existential, and not a chance accidental one, then we shall have theological proof that the mode of existence of the person of the Risen One is in time and space. So we must ask this question 'Where?'

'Where does he stand?' He stands *pro me*. He stands in my place, where I should stand and cannot. He stands on the boundary of my existence, beyond my existence, but still for me. This expresses the fact that I am separated from the 'I' that I should be by a boundary which I am unable to cross. This boundary lies between me and myself, between the old 'I' and the new 'I'. I am judged in my encounter with this boundary. At this place I cannot stand alone. Here Christ stands, in the centre, between me and myself, between the old existence and the new. So Christ is at the same time my own boundary and my rediscovered centre, the centre lying both between 'I' and 'I' and between 'I' and God. The boundary can only be known as a boundary from beyond the boundary. In Christ man knows it and thus at the same time finds his new centre.

The nature of the person of Christ is to be temporally and spatially in the centre. The one who is present in Word, sacrament and community is in the centre of human existence, history and nature. It is part of the structure of his person that he stands in the centre. If we turn the question 'Where?' back into the question 'Who?', the answer is, Christ is the mediator as the one who is there *pro me*. That is his nature and his mode of existence. He is in the centre in three ways; in being-there for men, in being-there for history and in being-there for nature.

1. Christ as the Centre of Human Existence

The fact that Christ is the centre of our existence does not mean that he is the centre of our personality, our thought and our feeling. Christ is our centre even when he stands on the periphery of our consciousness: he is our centre even when Christian piety is forced to the periphery of our being. The character of the statement about his centrality is not psychological, but ontological-theological. It does not relate to our personality, but to our being a person before God. The centre of the person is not demonstrable. The legitimacy of saying that Christ is our centre cannot be demonstrably confirmed. For it is a question of the centre that we believe to be in the sphere of the person.

In the fallen world, the centre is at the same time the boundary. Man stands between law and fulfilment. He has the law, but he cannot fulfil it. Now Christ stands where man fails towards the law. Christ as the centre means that he is the fulfilment of the law. So he is in turn the boundary and the judgment of man, but at the same time the beginning of his new existence, its centre. Christ as the centre of human existence means that he is man's judgment and his justification.

2. Christ as the Centre of History

Any attempt to give a philosophical vindication of the fact that Christ is the centre of history must be rejected. There can be no question of demonstrating that he is the consummation and the centre of religious and secular history. The statement that Christ is the centre of history has no more to be demonstrated than that he is the centre of our existence. Were Christ demonstrably shown to be the climax of all religions, that would still not prove that he is the centre. A comparison with other relative manifestations and a 'proof' which might possibly emerge of Christ being the centre of history would at best produce only a relative, not an absolute claim for Christ. All questions about an absolute claim are wrongly put. Comparisons with relative entities and proofs with relative questions do not result in an absolute. The question of the absolute is liberal and rational; it distorts the question which is intended here. The question of Christ as the centre and the boundary of history must be put in other terms.

History lives between promise and fulfilment. It bears within itself the promise, the divine promise, of becoming the womb of God's birth. The promise of a Messiah is alive everywhere in history. History lives in and from this expectation. That is its meaning, the coming of the Messiah. But history is related to this promise much as the individual man is related to the Law. As he cannot fulfil the law, neither can history fulfil its promise, because the promise is corrupted through sin. Man has the law only as it has been corrupted through sin. History has the promise only in a corrupt form. It lives from corrupted promises of 'fulfilled time', its *kairos*. History must reveal itself and make its own centre visible. It is driven to glorifying itself in its own Messiahs. A messiah as the centre of history is a respectable conception for the philosophy of history. But this promise remains unfulfilled. History is hindered by the impossibility of fulfilling corrupted messianic promises. It knows of the Messiah at its centre, but comes to grief on it.

Only in one place does the idea dawn that the Messiah cannot be the visible and demonstrable centre of history, but must be the hidden centre, appointed by God. Only in one place is there any progress against the stream of corrupt Messiahs. That is in Israel. With its prophetic hope, Israel stands alone among the peoples. And Israel becomes the place in which God fulfils his promise.

The fulfilment of this promise cannot be demonstrated in any way; it can only be proclaimed. That means that this Messiah Christ is at the same time both the destruction and the fulfilment of all the messianic expectations of history. He is their destruction in so far as the visible Messiah does not appear, but the fulfilment takes place in secret. He is their fulfilment in so far as God has really entered history and the expected one is now really there. The meaning of history is swallowed up by an event which takes place in the depth and secrecy of a man who is crucified. The meaning of history becomes evident only in the humiliated Christ.

Any other claim of history is judged and settled by this. History is here taken to its limit with its own promises. By nature it is at its end. By setting this boundary, however,

Christ at the same time again becomes its centre, its fulfilment. Christ stands where history as a whole should stand
before God. He is the *pro me* even for history. He is even
the mediator of history.

Since Christ is present in the church after the cross and
the resurrection, this church too must be understood as the
centre of history. It is the centre of a history which is made
by the state. Once again, this is a hidden centre of the
sphere of the state, not a demonstrable one. The church
proves its central place not by putting itself or allowing
itself to be put visibly in the centre of the state, by becoming,
say, a state church. It does not prove its relationship to
the state by its visible position in the sphere of the state. It
is the hidden meaning and promise of the state; it judges
and justifies the state in its nature. The nature of the state
is to bring a people nearer to its fulfilment by an action
which creates law and order. The messianic claim secretly
indwells the idea of the state's creating order.

Just as the church is the centre of the state, so too it is
its boundary. It is the boundary of the state in that with
the cross it proclaims the break-up of all human orders.
Just as it knows and believes that the law was fulfilled in
the cross, so too it also believes that the order of the state
was fulfilled in it too. The church does not institute a new
law with this knowledge of the cross and the preaching of it,
according to which the state has to act, but it proclaims
that by God's intervention in history and his death through
history the order of the state has finally been broken up and
dissolved, yet at the same time ultimately affirmed and
fulfilled.

As a result, the relationship between state and church
has been a new one since the cross. There has been a state
in the proper sense only as long as there has been a church.
The state has its proper origin since and with the cross (like

the church), in so far as this cross destroys and fulfils and affirms its order.

Christ is present to us in a double form, as church and as state. But this is true only for us, who receive him as Word and sacrament and community, for us, who, after the cross, must see the state in the light of Christ. The state is the rule of God 'with his left hand' (Luther WA 36, 385, 6-9; WA 52, 26, 20-26). As long as Christ was on earth he was the rule of God. When he was crucified, the rule broke into two, one by his right hand and one by the left hand of God. Now his rule can be known only as twofold, as church and as state. But the whole Christ is present to his church. And this church is the hidden centre of the state. The state need not know that the church is at its centre, but in fact it lives from this centre and cannot continue without it.

Christ as the centre of history is the mediator between the state and God, in the form of the church. Similarly, as the centre of history he is the mediator between this church and God. For he is also the centre of this church, and only because he is can it be the centre of history.

3. Christ as the Mediator between God and Nature

There has been little consideration of this question in Protestant theology hitherto.

Christ is *the* new creature. He thus shows all other creatures to be old creatures. Nature stands under the curse which God has laid on Adam's ground. It was originally the created Word of God, proclaiming the Word freely. As fallen creation, however, it is now dumb, in thrall under the guilt of men. Like history, nature suffers from the loss of its meaning and its freedom. It longs for a new freedom.

Nature is not reconciled, like man and history, but it is redeemed for a new freedom. Its catastrophes are the dull will to make itself free, to prove its power over men and to be a new creature in its own right, to create itself anew.

In the sacraments of the church, the enslaved old creation is made free for its new freedom. As the centre of human existence and of history, Christ is the fulfilment of the unfulfilled law, i.e. its reconciliation. But nature is a creature under the curse, not under guilt, for it has no freedom. So nature finds not reconciliation, but its redemption, in Christ as its centre. This redemption which takes place in Christ is again not demonstrable, it cannot be proved, but it is proclaimed. The word of preaching is that enslaved nature is redeemed in hope. A sign of this is given where, in the sacraments, elements of the old creation have become elements of the new creation. In the sacraments they are freed from their dumbness and proclaim directly to the believer the new creative Word of God. They no longer need man's interpretation. Enslaved nature does not utter the Word of creation directly to us. But the sacraments speak. In the sacrament, Christ is the mediator between nature and God, and stands for all creatures before God.

To sum up, we must continue to stress that Christ is indeed the centre of human existence, the centre of history and now, too, the centre of nature; but these three aspects can be distinguished only in the abstract. In fact, human existence is always history, always nature as well. As fulfiller of the law and liberator of creation, the mediator acts for the whole of human existence. He is the same, who is intercessor and *pro me*, and who is himself the end of the old world and the beginning of the new world of God.

The Historical Christ

The Historical Christ

I. ACCESS TO THE HISTORICAL CHRIST

We have so far spoken of the present Christ; but this present-historical (*geschichtliche*) Christ is the same person as the historical (*historische*) Jesus of Nazareth. Were this not so, we would have to say with Paul that our faith is vain and an illusion. The church would be deprived of its substance. There can be no isolation of the so-called historical (*historische*) Jesus from the Christ who is present now.

The attempt of liberal theology to distinguish a synoptic Jesus from a Pauline Christ is historically and dogmatically doomed to failure. Dogmatically, for if this separation of Jesus from Christ were possible, the proclamation of the church would become an illusion. Historically, because liberal theology up to 1900 can be described as an indirect, unintentional, and therefore all the more impressive, confirmation of the need for a dogmatic basis. The results of liberal theology are its own destruction. They make room for the assertion already made, that Jesus is the Christ.

Liberal theology stands and falls first of all by the separation of Jesus from the Christ. The Christ is Jesus declared divine by the community in a burst of enthusiasm. Jesus is Christ not in his nature and not in his person, but in his effect on others. A clear distinction must then be made between Jesus in his nature and Jesus in the eyes of the community. So ran the logic of liberal theology. The consequence was the quest for the historical Jesus. Scientific investigation had to discover the hard core of the historical Jesus and dispose of Jesus as the Christ. The result did not live up to expectations. Liberal theology itself was destroyed by this undertaking. It was impossible to write an historically credible life of Jesus. Wrede's and Schweitzer's books appeared (W. Wrede, *Über Aufgabe und Methode der sogenannten neutestamentlichen Theologie*, 1897, and *Das Messiasgeheimnis in den Evangelien*, 1901; Schweitzer, *Die Geschichte der Leben-Jesu-Forschung*, 1906). Schweitzer came to the conclusion that a quest for the historical Jesus is an impossibility in itself. Wrede made it clear that a purely historical Jesus is inconceivable, because the synoptic gospels themselves, which contain the earliest material, are already based on the presupposition of the 'faith of the community'. It is impossible to get behind the faith in the *Kyrios Christos* to a purely historical Jesus.

The end of liberal theology means two things:

a. negatively, it means the collapse of its own presupposition that Jesus was someone other than the Christ;

b. positively, it means that from now on the *historical* interpretation of the New Testament can justifiably be pursued only after serious consideration of the presupposition that Jesus is the proclaimed *Kyrios Christos*

Two courses are open: either to remain on the historical plane and to treat the *Kyrios-Christos* cult as one of a number of similar cults; or, to pass from historical to dogmatic study. The historical plane has shown that Jesus cannot be separated from the Christ. It is no longer possible to contrast a religion of Jesus, in which only the Father plays a role, with a cult of Christ. Thus any theology which makes this distinction its starting point is impossible. The result is all the more striking, because dogmatic and historical scholarship were opposed from the beginning. Finally, however, with Wrede, the covenant between history and dogmatics has been concluded. Historical investigation has again quarried from the New Testament the presuppositions of dogmatics: the unity of the present and of the historical (*geschichtliche*) Christ, the unity of the Jesus of proclamation and the Jesus of history.

In his book, *Der sogenannte historische Jesus und der geschichtliche biblische Christus*, which appeared in 1892, Martin Kähler made two observations:

a. the quest of the historical Jesus took a false course;

b. the historical (*geschichtliche*) Christ is the Christ of preaching.

Dogmatics was thus saying what historical studies later acknowledged. Now a time will come when scholars are interested in dogmatic studies, which seek to understand not so much the divine influences of Jesus as the divinity of Jesus Christ.

But what if at a later stage historical criticism again questions dogmatic statements, perhaps makes them impossible, because it must again change its conclusions? To what extent is dogmatic statement dependent on historical confirmation?

Two things must be said here:

a. Dogmatics needs to be certain of the historicity of Jesus Christ, i.e. of the identity of the Christ of preaching with the Jesus of history;

b. We must enquire how dogmatics can be certain of this historicity.

Can historical investigation support dogmatic statements? Do we have access to the historical figure of Jesus only through history? In that case history would have to be regarded as *historia sacra*. But that will not do, either empirically or theologically. Or can we have direct access to Jesus Christ apart from history? In other words, how is the church absolutely sure of the historical fact?

It is a characteristic of historical scholarship that it never reckons with the individual fact as the absolute. Nothing ever depends on the individual fact. Each individual fact has some element of chance to it. Its absolute necessity can never be demonstrated. But the historically (*geschichtlich*) fortuitous fact of the life and death of Jesus must be of basic and absolute significance for the church. If he did not live, the church is doomed. If the church is not sure of this, it is at an end. So how am I sure of the historical fact of 'Jesus Christ'? Historical investigation and its methods are manifestly transcended here. These questions might be dealt with in the following way:

a. Historical investigation can never maintain an absolute negative because it can never maintain an absolute positive. Absolute negation and absolute affirmation both transform history into *historia sacra*. So history can never absolutely deny the existence of Jesus Christ. It can only cast doubt on it or make it appear improbable. As a subject for historical investigation, Jesus Christ remains an uncertain phenomenon; his historicity can neither be affirmed nor denied with absolute certainty. History has no absolute authority to prove dogmatic statements impossible.

b. Absolute certainty about an historical fact can never be acquired by itself. It remains a paradox. Nevertheless it is constitutive for the church. That means that for the church an historical fact is not past, but present; that what is uncertain is the absolute, what is past is present, and what is historical (*das Geschichtliche*) is contemporaneous (Kierkegaard). Only where this contradiction is tolerated is the historical absolute. This statement, that what is historical is contemporaneous, what is hidden is open, is made possible only where what is historical, what is hidden, has made itself contemporaneous and open, i.e. in faith in the miracle of God in the resurrection of Jesus Christ.

There is thus no way from historical investigation to absoluteness. There is no absolute ground of faith in history. But from where does faith receive its sufficient ground to know, when history is uncertain? There is only the witness of the Risen One to himself, through which the church bears witness to him as the Historical One. By the miracle of his presence in the church he bears witness to himself here and now as the one who was historical then.

Historical access to the historical Jesus is not binding on faith. Historical certainty is by no means unique with Jesus; it is no more than any other encounter with a figure of the past. We can have 'hours with Christ' just as we can have hours with Goethe. Nor is it a matter of a mystical union with an historical figure; this is a person who bears witness to himself. It is not even, as Wilhelm Herrmann thought, that the bewildered conscience finds an encounter with Jesus in the inner life, and through this encounter forms its conviction of the historical figure of Jesus. The Risen One himself creates belief and so points the way to himself as the Historical One. From here, faith needs no confirmation from history. The confirmation of historical investigation is irrelevant before the self-attestation of Christ in the present. In faith, history is known in the light of eternity. That is the direct access of faith to history.

But does this not open the way for all sorts of heresy? That is not so, because the self-attestation of Jesus Christ is none other than that which is handed down to us by Scripture, and it comes to us in no other way than by the Word of Scripture. We have in the first place to do with a book, which we find in the secular sphere. It must be read and interpreted. It is meant to be read with all the means of historical and philological criticism. Even the believer has to do this soberly and objectively. At times we are involved in the problematic situation of having to preach about a saying which we know from philological and historical criticism never to have been spoken in its present form by Jesus. In the exegesis of Scripture we find ourselves on very uncertain ground. So we may never stick at one point, but must move over the whole of the Bible, from one place to another, just as a man can only cross a river covered in ice floes if he does not remain standing on one particular floe but jumps from one to another (Thurneysen).

There may be difficulties in preaching about a Word whose authenticity has been clearly denied by history. But verbal inspiration is a bad surrogate for the resurrection. It means the denial of the sole presence of the Risen One. It eternalizes history instead of seeing and recognizing history in the light of God's eternity. It fails in the attempt to level the difficult ground. The Bible also remains a book among books. We must be ready to admit the concealment in history and thus accept the course of historical criticism. But the Risen One encounters us right through the Bible with all its flaws. We must enter the straits of historical criticism. Its importance is not absolute, but at the same time it is not a matter of indifference. In fact it never leads to a weakening of faith but rather to its strengthening, as concealment in historicity is part of Christ's humiliation.

The historicity of Jesus Christ thus comes under the twofold aspect of history and faith. Both aspects are closely associated. The Jesus of history has humbled himself; the Jesus who cannot be grasped by history is the subject of faith in the resurrection.

In what follows, we are to consider the historical form of the Risen One. The ancient church began with the historical Jesus Christ and neglected the present and risen Christ. This goes without saying. But we have lost this presupposition. So we have had to deal here first of all with his presence.

II. CRITICAL OR NEGATIVE CHRISTOLOGY

Here we are concerned with that part of christology in which the incomprehensibility of the person of Jesus Christ is to be made comprehensible. Our understanding here, however, should consist in leaving this element of incomprehensibility as it is. The incomprehensible cannot be changed into something comprehensible; it is rather a matter of rejecting any attempts at such a transformation. Critical christology aims at delimiting the sphere within which this element of incomprehensibility must be allowed to remain. It will be critical because it must test any statement about Christ with regard to this limitation. The results of critical christology are of a negative character, as it establishes and decrees what may *not* be said about Christ.

Positive christology can be developed accordingly. But any attempt at a positive christology must continually be subject to criticism. Historically, this was expressed in the fact that the councils always produced a negative, restrictive christology. The first steps towards a positive christology, on the other hand, have been made from time to time by individual theologians. The councils marked out the limits to which these attempts might go by their criticism. These conciliar contributions make up the content of critical theology. Positive theology, however, did it the service of forcing a sharper definition of its limits from time to time. The progress from council to council was brought about by those men who had appeared in the meanwhile and produced a positive christology. Critical theology is a matter for the official church; it has its place in the teaching authority of the church's councils. Positive christology in practice happens permanently through the proclamation of the church, and has its place in preaching and in the sacraments. The limits laid down by the ancient church reveal their tremendous significance in our day.

If critical christology is thus concerned with marking out limits, that means that it is concerned with the concept of heresy. We have lost the concept of heresy today because there is no longer a teaching authority. This is a tremendous catastrophe. The present ecumenical councils are not quite councils because the word heresy has been removed from their vocabulary. But there can be no confession without saying, 'In the light of Christ, this is true and this is false.' The concept of heresy belongs necessarily and irrevocably with that of the confession. The doctrine of a confessional church must be contrasted with false doctrine. The Augsburg Confession says clearly: the church condemns.

We should note here that the concept of heresy emerges from the brotherliness of the church and not from a lack of love. A man acts as a brother towards his fellow only if he does not withhold the truth from him. If I do not tell my neighbour the truth, I treat him as a heathen. If I speak the truth to someone of another opinion, then I am showing him the love that I owe him.

1. The Docetic Heresy

The docetic heresy attempts to make Christ's incarnation comprehensible by understanding Jesus Christ as a manifestation of the Godhead in history. Christ's manhood is a cloak and a veil; it is the means which God uses to speak to men. It is not, however, of the essence of the matter. Jesus, the man, is a transparent envelope for God. This heresy is as old as Christianity itself and it still flourishes today. Two elements give it its force:

a. An abstract idea of God. That is, a doctrine of God which can take no account of men and which defines his nature independently of them. The Godhead is already known before it is revealed. The truth is already known as a supra-historical, absolute idea. If God is thus imagined as idea, then Christ must be understood as the manifestation of this idea, and not as individuality. This heresy must take no account of the humanity in Christ. If God wills to encounter man, he leaves the world of the idea and enters the world of phenomena. The form he seeks for himself is inessential compared with its nucleus. The origin of this thought lies in the Greek antithesis of idea and phenomenon. Any this-worldly phenomenon is inessential compared with what exists in the world of ideas. The docetic heresy is the typical heresy of Greek thought. It is pagan thought *par excellence.* It has one opponent: Jewish thought. Jewish thought is not based on the contrast between idea and phenomenon, so docetism could find no place in it. Instead of the docetic, the Ebionite heresy developed in Judaism.

b. One particular conception of redemption underlies the docetic heresy. In the ancient church, it was said that man's nature had to be redeemed by Christ. It is the individual man in his individuality who has fallen. In Schelling's words, individuality is sin. Man is meant to be restored to his nature from captivity in his individuality. This nature is common to all men. Redemption is being freed from individuality and being restored to one's essence (=nature). This redemption restores the unity and original condition of the whole human race. 'Man, become what you are' (Angelus Silesius). Here Silesius was saying what had been said in the ancient church and what was later said by Idealism. Now if the Bible spoke of Christ being incarnate to redeem us, on docetic presuppositions this meant that God had taken the nature and essence of man, but not man with his individuality. By taking the nature of man he has redeemed him for his original nature from individuality, which is sin. But this raised the question how it was possible to speak of a full incarnation if God has taken man's 'nature', but not his individuality. The accent, however, fell on this omission in the interest of saving God from falling victim to sin as individual man, thus making redemption impossible.

This is where the teaching of *Apollinarius of Laodicea* began. He was one of the most brilliant and most successful dogmatic theologians of the ancient church. He taught that while the Logos assumed human nature with *sarx* and *psyche*, he did not assume the *nous*. By *nous* he understood the element which makes man an individual, a person with his spiritual individuality. The incarnation is thus an appearance of God in human nature without the characteristics of this nature which make up the individual. There is no *nous* in Jesus; its place is taken by the Logos. The full incarnation of God did not therefore take place. This is a *dokein*. This subtle docetism was soon detected, and the teaching of Apollinarius was condemned as being heretical. For if the incarnation was not complete, then it did not take place at all and redemption was jeopardised. The ancient church therefore recognized that the Incarnate took *sarx*, *psyche* and *nous*.

Once this was assured, the problem arose how this individual person could be God. Could the complete unity of person in Christ still be preserved? Was there not then a Jesus *and* a Christ in the incarnate? Although ancient orthodoxy had recognized the *nous* in Christ in the course of christological discussion, it laboured under the idea that this could imply a Jesus who was man not only by his nature but also in his fallen individuality. An expedient was sought and found in a postponement of the problem. Although the incarnation was taught in such a way that *sarx, psyche* and *nous* seemed to be included together, Jesus was not allowed his own hypostasis. He had no mode of existence of his own; his proper existence was the existence of God. This is what was meant by the doctrine of *enhypostasia*. God and man were again separated, each into his own hypostasis. So the person of Jesus was now to be enhypostatic with the divine hypostasis. But with this doctrine of enhypostasia, which was meant to prevent the separation of God and man in Christ, the dogmatics of the ancient church already found itself fighting a rearguard action against docetism. The latter had already slipped back into the orthodox dogma of the ancient church in a refined form. In the denial of the hypostasis, docetism had retreated to a final position and held it. Brunner overlooks this in *The Mediator* when he regards the doctrine of *enhypostasia* as a good insight of the ancient church and makes it his own. Luther says, 'You should point to the whole man Jesus and say, "That is God." '

The reason for the constant deflection of ancient christology into docetism lies in its conception of redemption, in which the nature (essence) and personal character (individuality) of man are differentiated. The abstract doctrine of God and the idea of redemption have the same presupposition, the contrast of idea and phenomenon which we have already mentioned. The idea is substance, the phenomenon is accident; Christ the God is substance, Jesus the man is accident. The docetic doctrine of the incarnation is moulded by a philosophical presupposition. Anyone who does not free himself from this presupposition (idea-phenomenon) will seek in vain to escape docetism, whether of a cruder or more subtle kind.

The Gnostics Basilides and Valentinus represent the earliest form of docetism.

Basilides teaches that there was no union of the *primogenitus nous Christus* with the phenomenon Jesus. Jesus was merely the 'accidental' basis for the Christ; the union was transitory and already dissolved before the crucifixion. Christ had already gone to heaven before the crucifixion, and made a mock of the devil. Jesus was a real man and the 'accidental' starting-point for the æon of Christ. *Valentinus* and his pupil *Apelles* teach that the body of Christ was not born of man, but was a heavenly body. It simply passed through Mary. *Satornilus* went so far as to say that Christ did not have a body at all, that he was not born, and suffered only in phantom form. All three have in common a complete indifference to Jesus; he is the chance phenomenon; it is the idea and the way in which it is displayed which must be grasped. Whether it was Jesus in whom the idea was displayed, and who Jesus was, does not matter at all.

The ancient church opposed these docetists with all its strength. It was concerned to proclaim an event and not an idea of redemption, and it held fast to the incarnation. The real man had to be redeemed. For the church, everything depended on the historicity of Jesus Christ. But attempts were made to bring the historicity of this Jesus Christ into line with the ideas of God and redemption prevailing at the time. So qualifications had to be made. The doctrine of *enhypostasia* stands at the end of the church's struggle with docetism. It remains an irreducible remnant in the orthodox dogmatics of the ancient church, a tribute to the presuppositions of docetic thought. Even at the end, the incarnation was still thought of as an accident to the substance in orthodox formulæ. Nevertheless, the enemy had been detected and mentioned by name. Docetism had been condemned as a deviation.

Docetism has clearly reappeared in more recent Protestant theology, though of course in a different form. Interest now lies in the historical Jesus. A speculative concept of history has taken the place of the old speculative idea of God. Now history has become the support of particular religious ideas and values. History is a manifestation of supra-historical ideas. One of its values is, for example, the idea of the religious personality of man with the 'constant force of his consciousness of God' (Schleiermacher). Jesus is the embodiment or support for this idea in history.

Why is that docetic? Because a particular religious idea is first held and then applied to the historical Jesus. The picture of man obtained from a particular concept of history is projected on to Jesus. The decisive thing is that here, too, the incarnation has simply become the means to an end.

This is clearly the case in the christology of *Albrecht Ritschl*. He says that Christ is designated as God only through the value judgment of the community. The community addresses him as God, and as a result of this verdict Christ is God. Ritschl distinguishes judgments of fact from value judgments. The community has a range of values. With this it approaches the figure of the historical Jesus and applies it to him or finds it realized in him. The values which are embodied in Jesus of Nazareth are, among others, grace, fidelity, lordship over the world. The man Jesus is the manifestation of such values.

From here on, the whole of liberal theology must be seen in the light of docetic christology. It understands Jesus as the support for or the embodiment of particular ideas, values and doctrines. As a result, the manhood of Jesus

Christ is in the last resort not taken seriously, although it is this very theology which speaks so often of the man. It passes over his manhood and brings Jesus more than ever into the field of speculation and reconstruction. The understanding of the man as the support for a particular idea bypasses his real existence. It confuses the real man with an ideal man and makes him a symbol. This docetism found its most brilliant form in Hegel's *philosophia sacra*. Here the relationship of idea and phenomenon was brought to perfection. Now the phenomenon is no longer an accident, but the necessary form of the idea. On the basis of a modalistic doctrine of the Trinity, the incarnation for Hegel is no longer a semblance but an essential and necessary manifestation of God in history. It is an element of God's being what he appears. Only as the one who is historical is God God. But this very 'necessity' of the incarnation is the dangerous part. For here something is made into a principle which cannot and may not be a principle. God becomes man—that is the very thing which *in principle* is inconceivable. Otherwise we do not have the real man, but an idea of man. God's incarnation is no necessity which may be derived from God himself. If idea and phenomenon may perhaps be related one to another under the principle of some necessity, this is never the case with God and man, God and history. In reality, this thesis fails to do justice to man in his historicity. The incarnation is the incomprehensible, the impossible; it remains in God's freedom; it is God's coming which cannot be deduced in any way whatsoever.

Biedermann, who is a disciple of Hegel, then proclaimed the dissolution of christological dogma. He said that the form of Jesus of Nazareth was to be replaced. Christ was the fulfilment and the representative of a principle, the principle of Sonship. Even though Biedermann denied it, the humanity and historicity of Christ had again become an accident of the divine substance. Docetism had entered the Protestant camp in pure culture.

The church must reject docetism in any form because docetism challenges Christ's being for the community. Along with it, the church will reject any form of Greek-idealistic thought in so far as this works with the distinction of idea and phenomenon. Idealism removes the first principle of all theology, that God really became man of his own free grace. Christ did not of necessity realize a divine or even a human principle. The proximity of any docetism to idealism or to rationalism is, of course, part of its fascination.

2. The Ebionite Heresy

The Ebionite heresy does not derive from a pagan philosophy for which the dogma of the incarnation is folly. For Ebionitism, faith in the cross is rather a scandal, an affront and a dishonour to God. It attempts to get round the fact that this folly of God is his wisdom. So in its own way it tries to make God's folly in the world wise. But even here, man cannot make it wiser than it is. God himself surrendered his honour, so man cannot restore it to him.

Ultimately, only this approach is worth contrasting with that of pagan idealism. It has its roots in Israelite thought. The Ebionite heresy is the heresy of Jewish Christianity, which never surrenders the background of its strict mono-theistic belief in God. True, it attempts to keep the mystery of the incarnation by understanding it as the promotion of a man to divine honour, but to put another God alongside the one God is, for the Ebionite, blasphemy. There can be

no second God. But it will not have Jesus as a manifestation
of God on earth either. Israelite thought knows no metamorphosis of God, as does Greek-docetic thought. The
creator cannot transform himself into his creature. Jesus
remains God's creature, a particular man. Jesus, the particular man: this is the advance of the Ebionite heresy over
docetism, that it holds fast to the God of the Old Testament,
who is no God of metamorphoses. It cannot, however,
recognize the relationship of God to this man Jesus in an
identity of being, but only in a qualified relationship. So
first of all it rejects a supernatural birth, even if it recognizes
Jesus as *Kyrios*, and singles him out for special honour;
secondly, it disputes the pre-existence of Christ and thirdly,
utterly denies the real divinity of Jesus.

The baptism acquires a special significance. At his
baptism, Jesus is accepted as the Son of God who does the
will of God. The Spirit of God comes upon the mature,
pure man Jesus. He is not God in substance, but he receives
a special Sonship of God. There is a development in him.
He *is* not God, but he *becomes* 'God', and does so all the
more, the more strongly the Spirit takes possession of him.
The Jewish Christian sees this in the way that Jesus fulfils
the Law even to the extent of being obedient on the cross.
Designations of Jesus as Son of God alternate with those
which name him a prophet of truth. Jesus Christ is a man
elevated to divine status. But this must not be understood
to mean that he is like a Greek hero. The theme of pagan-
Greek thought (docetism) is a disregard for, and a removal
of, the boundary between creator and creature. The theme
of Israelite thought (Ebionitism) is the very preservation
of the distance between them. On the one side there is a
belief in the possibility of man's being perfected; on the
other there is a realization of his limitations. The Jewish-
Christian notion—Jesus is the man elevated to be Christ

and Son—and the Greek notion—Jesus is the man transformed into a demigod—seem to be very similar in the concept of the divinized man. But their origins are fundamentally different. Docetism and Ebionitism are often difficult to distinguish from each other. Nevertheless, the one heresy is interesting in removing, the other in preserving, the limitations of man. Because the Ebionite line often and easily blends with that of docetism, it is hard to follow in the history of dogma.

The Ebionite heresy is represented by the Monarchians. Their interest lies in the oneness of God. Their chief representative is *Paul of Samosata*. He qualifies the divinity of Jesus Christ and stresses his creatureliness. For him, the divinity of Christ is merely his voluntary association with the Father. The Holy Spirit is conceived of as an impersonal force at work in Jesus. The baptism is Jesus' calling to be Son of God. Jesus undergoes a development. The ancient church condemned the teaching of Paul of Samosata as heretical because of this qualification of the divinity of Jesus Christ.

Liberal theology was fond of referring to Paul of Samosata as a forerunner. True, there are analogies, but this reference to him is in fact unjustified. Liberal theology is, in essentials, not Ebionite, but docetic in nature. It begins from the infinite value of man. Its statements point in the direction of the genius and the hero. It is *A. Schlatter*, rather, who comes near to Ebionitism. Instead of praising the man with his infinite value, Ebionitism praises the obedient servant who sees God's honour as his own. With this servant, the salvation of mankind and the church is bound up. Despite its external similarity, Ebionitism is superior to docetic liberalism in that it keeps its eyes on the particular person Jesus, the real man. Salvation is not associated with an ideal picture, but with the servant. Ebionitism never forgets to consider the real man as well as the creator God. What it does not succeed in doing—and this, of course, is the decisive factor—is in finding a way from the real creator God to the real man, the servant. Christ's redeeming work is thus jeopardized and comes to nothing. Ebionitism cannot teach Jesus Christ as true man and true God at the same time, and so the church must condemn it.

To sum up: the concept of the incarnation must be defined negatively in such a way as to expose any attempt which interprets either the full manhood or the full Godhead of Jesus at the cost of qualifying either one or the other. In christology, the humanity of God and the divinity of the man are to be held together at the risk of destroying the rationality of the exposition. Christology must be defined positively in such a way that it follows a middle course between the docetic and the Ebionite heresies. The 'How?' questions of docetic and Ebionite christology must be replaced by the question 'Who?'

3. The Monophysite and Nestorian Heresies

1. The question of the divinity of Jesus Christ is raised here. How can the person of God be conceived if he became a real man in Jesus Christ? In the development of the doctrine of the God-manhood of Christ the monophysite and Nestorian heresies took shape.

The significance of the person of Jesus for saving history demanded that the saving-historical event took place within human nature. The monophysites were concerned that this human nature, i.e. our nature, should be wholly assumed by God and thus divinized. *Physike henosis* (the union in one nature) became the slogan the one nature of God the Lord incarnate. In that case, Christ is not to be understood as an individual man; he slipped on human nature like a garment. True, he suffered, thirsted and wept like men, but he did this because he *willed* to, not because it was his nature. Everything depended on a union being achieved between the divine and the human nature in Christ. For if God's nature was not manifested in ours, how could our nature be redeemed, made whole and divinized?

This, however, was in contrast to the biblical position. According to the Bible, Jesus was an individual man with all the properties and limitations of a man. He wept, trembled, and knew that he was not omniscient. So the Nestorians were concerned to preserve the biblical *datum* of the full manhood of Jesus Christ. Christ is the complete man. They saw themselves compelled to accept two separate natures in Christ, the divine nature remaining completely separate from the humanity. One, they said, was capable of suffering, the other was not. A substantial union of the two natures in Christ was an insult to the creator. It was only possible to speak of a voluntary union with God. The distance from God was maintained, and confusion or metamorphosis was obviated. But the Nestorians omitted to notice that despite the way in which the humanity of Jesus was taken seriously, it was now no longer possible to speak of an incarnation of *God*, if the difference of the natures was asserted as it was. In contrast to the monophysite concern, the saving-historical element was left completely on one side. How was human nature to be redeemed, if it was not permissible to believe in a unity in Christ?

The controversy led to a passionate radicalization of the two positions and revealed the insoluble dilemma of the doctrine of the two natures. The monophysites were impelled by a deeper seriousness, the Nestorians by a greater fidelity to the Bible. On the one hand, there was the mystery of a unity of the divine and human natures, on the other, the matter-of-factness of a clear separation. On the one hand there was the mystery of the unity; on the other, the rationality of the duality. On the one hand, there was the divinization of man; on the other, the ethos of the servant who elevated himself, conforming to the will of God. On the one hand, there was the question of salvation; on the other that of truth. On the one hand, there was passionate ardour, zeal and dogged tenacity; on the other, the need for clarity. On the one hand, there were priestly figures like Athanasius, though of course he did not explicitly belong among the monophysites; on the other, laity, ascetics and theologians like Arius. Radicalization and controversy were inevitable.

The climax came when the monophysite Eutyches of Constantinople confessed, 'My God is not of the same nature as I am. He is not individual man, but human by nature. His body was not *soma anthropou* but *anthropinon*.' This radical statement both defended the one nature and settled its fate. The Nestorians struck back on the other hand by refusing to Mary the title *Theotokos*.

These were the boundaries within which the ancient church had to find its statement about the *Mysterium Christi*. On the one hand it had to reject the heresy of monophysitism because there the human nature in Christ was finally swallowed up by the divine and because it ended in a speculation on the nature of God and man, ultimately expressing the identity of God and man. Monophysitism remained influential in medieval philosophy. On the other hand, the ancient church had to repudiate the heresy of Nestorianism because in it the manhood and the Godhead of Christ were ultimately so divorced that it was no longer possible to conceive of a unity of the person of Jesus Christ and to speak seriously of an incarnation of God.

The Chalcedonian Definition of 451, which produced the classic formulation of the doctrine of the God-manhood of Jesus Christ, was directed against these two particular heresies: 'One and the same Christ, in two natures, *without confusion and without change*,' not to be thought of as a metamorphosis of God, against monophysitism; '*without division and without separation*,' against the Nestorians.

The Chalcedonian Definition was concerned with the complete divine and complete human nature of Christ, with the one Jesus Christ with two natures.

What did the formula of Chalcedon say? It stated the *a priori* impossibility and impermissibility of taking the divinity and humanity in Jesus Christ side by side or together or as a relationship of objectifiable entities. Simple negations remain. No positive pattern of thought is left to explain what happens in the God-man Jesus Christ. Thus the mystery is left as a mystery and must be understood as such. Access is reserved solely for faith. All thought forms are cut short. After the decision of Chalcedon it is no longer permissible to objectify the divinity and the manhood in Christ and to distinguish them from each other as entities. We cannot form a concept of God and then draw boundaries within it. The Chalcedonian Definition has wrongly been charged with being the expression or the basis of scholastic theology. It has wrongly been said to be a compromise solution after a theologians' squabble. After the Chalcedonian Definition, the theologian who is concerned with christology must keep within the conceptual tension of this negative formula and preserve it. It came about, as Schweitzer's view has it, '*Dei providentia et hominum confusione.*' Its peculiar character lies in the way in which it cancels itself out. In other words, it shows the limitations of the concepts it employs simply by using them. It speaks of 'natures', but it expresses the facts in a way which demonstrates the concept of 'natures' to be an inappropriate one. It works with concepts which it declares to be heretical formulas unless they are used paradoxically and in contradiction. It brings the concept of substance which underlies the relationship of the natures to a climax and does away with it. From now on it will no longer be permissible to say anything about the *substance* of Jesus Christ. Speculation about 'natures' is at an end; the notion of substance is superseded. If a development of the Chalcedonian Definition were conceivable, it could not be a development in thought about the relationship of the natures; it would be something else which has still to be mentioned. The Chalcedonian Definition is an objective, but living, statement which bursts through all thought-forms. In its negative formulations it is the model of a theological conciliar statement. Clearly and paradoxically, it is a vivid expression of what from now on is orthodox doctrine: Christ is one person in two natures.

2. The Chalcedonian Definition led to a great development within the Protestant tradition. The orthodox formula, that Christ is one person in two natures, was held to be valid, but how could it be interpreted further in Chalcedonian terms, in such a way that both the soteriological theme and the biblical side had equal prominence? The account of the natures had to include the fact that God is fully man. But how can Jesus of Nazareth be omnipotent and present, and yet merely man? How could God suffer in Christ? How could he be otherwise than omniscient and omnipotent in him? The answers to these questions had to take a form that neither jeopardized the Godhead of Christ nor obliterated his manhood.

In conjunction with the thought-pattern of the two natures in one person, Lutheranism developed the doctrine of the *communicatio idiomatum* or the *unio hypostatica*, the most acute speculation which its theology reached in the christological question.

In this doctrine, Lutheranism held fast to the presupposition that the integrity of both natures in Christ must be preserved, the divine nature in its immutability and essential eternity, the human nature in its mutability and finite transitoriness. Before their integral unity in one person, however, they were first conceived of in isolation from one another. So the procedure which the Chalcedonian Definition had prohibited was still being followed. The human nature, for example, did not keep its full human character from the beginning in the doctrine of the sinlessness of the human nature of Jesus.

The first expression of consequence ran (once the isolation had been presupposed): the two natures combine themselves in a *unitio* to form a *unio*. This *unio* is characterized by the fact that the divine nature—*mere active*—governs the human nature—*mere passive*. The divine nature is active and person-forming; it suffuses the passive human nature as fire does iron. The result is the *unio personalis*. This is from now on the real and indissoluble conjunction of the two natures. God the Logos is no longer there except in the flesh. He is only there as the Incarnate, inseparably bound up with man.

This *unio* of Logos and sarx means the mutual *communio naturarum*, their complete *perichoresis* (John 1.14; Col. 2.9; Heb. 2.14). If the *unio personalis* expressed the unity of God and man, the *communio naturarum* expresses the uniting of the natures of Godhead and manhood.

The *communio naturarum* finds its expression in the doctrine of the *propositiones personales*. This means that the particular characteristics of each individual nature can also be predicated of the particular characteristics of the other. Thus it can and must be said that the man (Jesus) is God and that

God is man. But it cannot and may not be said that God-head is manhood or vice versa. So the particular characteristics of God and man are predicated each of the other, while the integrity of the natures remains preserved.

The conjunction of the two natures thus described finally makes possible the decisive feature, the *communicatio idiomatum* (Col. 2.9). It teaches the mutual participation and exchange of the individual properties of the natures. It is thought of in three ways:

a. The *genus idiomaticum* (*primum genus*). That means that what is true of one or other of the natures can be predicated of the person of the whole God-man. Thus 'Jesus is born' can also run, 'Christ, the Son, God, is born', or 'Jesus suffers' can also run, 'Christ, the Son of God, God, suffers'.

b. The *genus apotelesmaticum* (*tertium genus*). The saving acts which are performed by the person of Jesus Christ can also be predicated of the individual natures. 'Jesus Christ makes us pure from sin' can also run, 'The blood of Christ makes us pure'. Both natures share in this office of Christ (1 John 1.7).

c. The *genus maiestaticum* (*secundum genus*). According to the two *genera* under *a* and *b* we can now also go on to speak of the relationship of the two natures one to another. Do the two natures of Godhead and manhood stand in an immediate relationship to one another, and if so, how? For Luther, the explanation of this *genus* is the decisive thing. *Genus maiestaticum* means that the predicates of the eternal Godhead may and must also be expressed of the human nature. We must therefore say, 'Jesus is omnipotent, Jesus is present'. What we have here is the *est* of eucharistic doctrine. Even the humanity of Christ must have its part in the doctrine of ubiquity.

The *genus maiestaticum* lies at the very heart of Lutheran christology. But at this point a conflict develops with biblical expressions. There is also a lurking danger of the recurrence of monophysitism, in that the manhood still becomes the Godhead, or the divine nature is almost transformed into the human nature. In the *Formula of Concord*, art. VIII 5, *De persona Christi*, we find: 'For we believe, acknowledge and teach both natures to be united personally, that is, in one person, and that this union is not such a conjunction and association that one nature has anything in common with the other personally, that is, for the sake of their personal union, just as, when one glues two planks together, neither gives anything to the other or takes it from the other. But here is the supreme community which God truly has with "man", from which personal union and the resulting supreme and inexpressible community everything derives that can be said and believed humanly of God and divinely of the man Christ, which union and community of natures the ancient teachers of the church have explained by the image of a fiery iron and of the union of body and soul in man!'

Reformed theologians energetically protested against this Lutheran christology and raised three objections to it:

a. The person of Christ thus described is no longer the figure of the Redeemer of whom the New Testament speaks. That figure is more immediate.

b. Lutheran thought here presupposes a change in God. God's being can never be man's being. Beings or natures remain separate; only the persons become one.

c. In the *genus maiestaticum*, Lutheran christology is in the last resort no longer speaking of the real humanity of Christ.

By way of a counter to Lutheran christology, Reformed theologians affirmed: True, the Logos has entered the flesh, but not in such a way that he is not also outside the flesh. The Logos remains in his trinitarian relationship and therefore also *extra carnem*. He does not enter into any necessary, indissoluble conjunction with the flesh. On the other hand, there is a development in Christ's human nature; it gradually becomes the perfect instrument of God and is anointed by the Holy Spirit. There is no *genus maiestaticum* and thus no divinization of the human nature. At the beginning there stands the sentence: *finitum incapax infiniti.* The natures are conjoined only by means of the person. In contrast to the doctrine of the *genus maiestaticum*, that means that what is said of the one nature, even of the person, cannot be said of the other nature.

But what did the Reformed theologians do about such New Testament passages as those which showed that Jesus had authority to forgive sins and to raise the dead? Here they introduced the concept of *alloiosis* (i.e. of change, altering). 'This is my body' is to be understood symbolically. Luther furiously resisted the concept of *alloiosis* as it did not allow the Word to stand as the Word. The Reformed theologians said that the Logos was everywhere, but that as God-man he was at a particular place.

Reformed christology attached great importance to the preservation of the divine and human natures intact; salvation depends on the integrity of the manhood of Christ. The Lutherans accused the Reformed theologians of imagining the relationship of the two natures to be like that of two planks glued together; and if there was no real union, then redemption was jeopardized. Were Christ only God through the anointing of the Holy Spirit, then in principle any man could become God. *Finitum* capax *infiniti, non per se sed per infinitum!*

The criterion for a decision must be sought in Scripture. Both the abstract duality of the natures and the abstract unity of the person are unbiblical. In fact, Luther can speak of the Godhead and manhood of Jesus as though they were one nature. He is concerned to understand the man-

hood of Jesus Christ as Godhead. The child in Bethlehem
is the one 'whom the whole world never embraced'. Out of
this there develops the doctrine of the *genus maiestaticum*,
which allows the human nature to be permeated by the
divine nature and to receive the attributes of the latter.
Luther is, in fact, in danger of failing to keep separate the
nature of Jesus and the nature of Christ.

3. The danger of arriving at a completely divinized man
or 'spiritualized flesh' was realized. Post-Lutheran orthodoxy sought to counter it by developing the doctrine of the
genus maiestaticum. It was concerned at this point to be able
to speak *in uno* both of the historical Jesus as he is depicted
by the synoptists and of the God-man redeemer Christ.
Christ experienced two different states, the *status exinani-
tionis* (the humiliation) and the *status exaltationis* (the exaltation). The subject of the *exinanitio* is, according to Lutheran
orthodoxy, not the one who is *becoming man* but the one who
has become man. In other words, the incarnation is not an
act of the Logos humbling himself. The incarnation remains,
even within the Trinity, eternal. The incarnation is a more
comprehensive concept than the humiliation. The Incarnate
One undergoes the humiliation of his own free will. The
humiliation is an attribute of the Incarnate, not an attribute
of the Logos as such. For the Reformed theologians, on the
other hand, the incarnation was itself the humiliation. For
them, the subject of the humiliation is the Logos, whereas
for the Lutherans it is the Logos incarnate.

Now what does this humiliation mean? It means restraint
from exercising the divine properties and powers through
the human nature for the duration of the earthly life of
Jesus Christ. The question then arises how this restraint is
to be understood. There are two possibilities:

a. There is a real renunciation, an actual evacuation of
the divine potentialities in the humiliation;

b. There is a concealment; the divine powers are no longer visible during the humiliation of Jesus.

So the doctrine of the two states is associated with the dispute between the *Kenoticists* (from Giessen, centred on Chemnitz, e.g. Mentzer) and the *Cryptics* (from Tübingen, centred on Brenz, e.g. Hafenreffer). They ask whether Christ shared in the universal lordship of God while he was on earth.

The cryptics are advocates of the theory of concealment (*krypsis chreseos*). They insist on the preservation of the identity of the God-man, as he is from eternity, with the Incarnate One, as he has made himself in the humiliation. Their concern is with the unity of person. If the Exalted One and the Humiliated One are not completely the same, all is lost. The one who must suffer, they say, is at the same time the one who must not suffer. The kenoticists objected: if that is so, then Christ did not really suffer and he did not really die. In that case it is all humbug and phantasy. The cryptic christology unwittingly finds itself in the realm of docetism.

The kenoticists are advocates of the theory of renunciation (*kenosis chreseos*). They insist that Phil. 2 deals with a real kenosis, that Christ really died after he had really suffered. Their concern is to preserve the human nature of Jesus Christ. True, it was not possible to talk of a *kenosis kteseos*, of a renunciation of the divine properties, but they could assume a renunciation of their use. Christ continually restrained himself from using his divine powers. The kenoticists find themselves approaching the *Extra-Calvinisticum*. They too endanger the reality of the renunciation and end up with a phantom procedure. They run the risk of splitting the person of Jesus Christ.

As the result of a compromise, the cryptics and the kenoticists finally united under an insignificant formula:

as the Humiliated One, Christ used his divine properties when he so willed and did not use them when he so willed. The question of the *ktesis* of the divine properties, the properly theological question of substance, is passed over and suppressed. Here and there, when God wills, man sees something of the divine properties illuminated. But this connection with miracle introduces another concept of faith. Faith here is bound up with the manifestation of God rather than with the hiddenness of the cross. The whole problem of christology is thus shifted on to another level. True, the unity of the person of Christ, the God-man, is preserved; but he is split into two different states. True, the identity of the God-man is preserved, but he is split into two figures, one concealed and one visible. But Christ is *always* the one person in two natures.

4. The doctrine of kenosis was taken up afresh in the nineteenth century. *Thomasius* and *Gess* revived it. They were prompted by the motive which underlies the Lutheran doctrine of condescension, even if the starting point had shifted. No longer is the incarnate God-man taken as the subject of the humiliation; this is transferred to the Logos himself. The sequence of events is no longer Logos-man-humiliation, but Logos-humiliation-man. The Logos, humbling himself, becomes man. The subject of the renunciation is the Logos, not the Logos incarnate. This change means a simplification in the picture of Christ. For these modern kenoticists the renunciation of the divine properties lies in the beyond, i.e. in a metaphysical act of the Logos. So the historical picture of Jesus Christ loses the inner violence of the suppression of his divine powers on which the earlier kenoticists insisted.

However, the question of the character of this renunciation still remained. Thomasius resorted to the expedient of distinguishing between the immanent and the relative properties of God. Those which belong to his absolute nature are immanent, those which speak of his relationship to the world are relative. For example, holiness, love, truth are immanent; omnipotence, omnipresence, onmiscience are relative. Now in Christ's case, the position is that he has taken and bears the immanent properties of God but not the relative ones. That means that the man Jesus Christ is not omnipresent, omniscient and omnipotent, but that he does have the truth, love and holiness of God at his disposal.

Gess did not hold with this expedient and went further. He said that in Christ God had renounced the whole of his being. He ceased to be God in Christ to find himself again as God in the gradually increasing self-consciousness of Jesus. On this, Biedermann remarked that it was the complete kenosis of understanding: it no longer meant anything at all.

The attempts of the modern kenoticists have failed for two reasons:

a. The divinity of Jesus Christ is not made comprehensible. It is qualified in that it becomes merely a part of man. But everything depends on the fact that God in his totality and omnipotent glory is this Incarnate One who meets us in Jesus. One of the first theological principles must continue to be that where God is he is fully there.

b. The humanity of Jesus Christ is not made comprehensible. The humanity of Christ is merely enlarged by a number of divine properties, so that Christ finally approaches the form of a demigod who lives on earth.

So the doctrine of kenosis tried to screw up the claims of the divine being until the divine and human natures finally fitted together in harmony. A concept of God and a concept of man were worked out and put together in such a way that they could not come apart. The smallest unevenness had catastrophic consequences. If the minutest thing did not fit the whole attempt failed. And in practice, the attempt did fail.

A comparison with the Chalcedonian Definition reveals that once again an attempt had been made to soften and balance contradictory and exclusive contrasts. It had been thought that one could define the divine and human natures *in abstracto* so that they fitted together. But this was only to fall victim to a simplification of the problem; the recognition of the real Jesus Christ had been made the recognition of a God-man construction. The prohibition against applying objectifying categories to the solution of the question of the God-man relationship had been violated.

Within the Lutheran doctrine of the *communicatio idiomatum*, the doctrine of kenosis was a necessary supplement to the *genus maiestaticum*.

Alongside this the kenoticists put the *genus tapeinoticum*. But with the doctrine of kenosis, Lutheran dogmatics was involved in the danger of rejecting the two natures doctrine of the Chalcedonian Definition by going beyond its negative stipulations in one place. A statement about Christ is constructed, i.e. the question 'How?' is answered instead of the bare question 'Who?' The Chalcedonian Definition had also given an answer to a question 'How?' But in its answer it was already clear that the question 'How?' had been superseded. In its negative insistence on contradictory opposites the Chalcedonian Definition has itself superseded the doctrine of two natures and in effect says that the question of Jesus Christ cannot be solved and that a demonstrable unity cannot be established with the concept of *nature*. This critical significance of the Chalcedonian Definition is to be taken further. This can only be done where any thought of the Godhead and manhood as something demonstrable has been superseded and the natures in isolation no longer form a starting point. The starting point is the fact that the man Jesus *is* the Christ, *is* God. This 'is' cannot be deduced. It is the presupposition of all thought, and cannot be constructed afterwards. After Chalcedon, the question can no longer be 'How can the natures be thought of as different and the person as one?' but strictly, 'Who is this man of whom it is testified that he is God?'

4. The Subordinationist and Modalistic Heresies

Here, within the statement that Jesus Christ is the Son of God, we are concerned with the *homoousia* of Jesus Christ with God. If it is impossible to speak of a *homoousia*, then once again everything is at stake. The concept of *homoousia* has undergone changes. Here it is to be understood not as *similarity* of being but as *identity* of being. Why is the statement that Christ has identity of being with the Father necessary and to be retained? Only in this way can the biblical testimony that God revealed himself in Christ be upheld. Only then is it possible to speak of the revelation of God. The concept of revelation presupposes that God is identical with himself in his revelation. Otherwise it is not strictly a question of revelation but of a manifestation, or an idea.

To say that God became man thus makes it necessary to say that Jesus Christ is identical in being with God. The attempt was made to settle for a *homoiousios*, but this formula was already almost that of Arius, who defended the *anomoios*.

For the *subordinationists*, everything depended on the preservation of the unity and monarchy of God. If it was necessary to assume a second God, this unity and monarchy would be attacked and destroyed. Jesus could therefore only be conceived of as God *anomoios* or at most *homoios*. Only in this way did it seem possible to preserve the unity of God. But this was done at the expense of revelation. For there is only revelation where it is possible to speak of the Son who is identical in being with the Father. And only in this revelation is the decision about my life made. So there was some skirmishing before the alternative: God's unity or God's revelation? This is where the error of any subordinationist christology lies. In its way, it did not really succeed in preserving the unity of God. It is this Either-Or which in truth attacks God's unity. For where Christ is understood as a man elevated to divine dignity, who in his nature is not God, but man, and who is revered as a demigod, the unity of God is called in question by this very demigod halfway between God and man. The way is opened for polytheism. Where God's unity is qualified for the sake of his revelation, this unity is destroyed. Modern Arianism, which honours Jesus as a genius and a hero, attacks God's unity as well as his revelation.

Modalism was an impressive attempt to think of God's unity and his revelation together. Christ is God's *prosopon*, i.e. the form in which God appears, the second of God's three forms (Schleiermacher). The modalists, however, must be asked whether they really take revelation seriously. Does God as a whole encounter man? Is even his unity preserved? Or is it still vitiated because we are bound to a phenomenon and not to the true God?

The concepts of revelation and monotheism demand each other. A qualified concept of revelation is the end of monotheism. Either Christ, as the revelation of God, is identical in being with God, or monotheism falls along with revelation. Neither subordinationists nor modalists take total revelation seriously and both offer false solutions, the former with the adopted Son, the latter with the Christ-

prosopon. The person of Christ is the indissoluble correlation of total revelation with identity of being. The formal christological principle of duality and unity is repeated: two natures and one person, two states and one God-man, two divine persons (Father and Son) and yet one God.

III. THE CONTRIBUTION OF CRITICAL CHRISTOLOGY

Critical christology is concerned with defining and guarding against a false Jesus Christ. Boundaries must be drawn to guard against both false theological content and inappropriate thought-forms.

Any sentences which make statements about Jesus Christ with unequivocal directness are to be designated as having a false theological content. Anyone who expresses the Godhead so clearly that it swallows up the manhood becomes a docetist. Anyone who expresses the manhood in such a way that the Godhead of Christ appears as an ultimate, virtuous, supreme human potentiality is condemned as an Ebionite. Anyone who stresses the unity of the person of Christ without at the same time giving expression to the duality of his Godhead and manhood is rejected as a monophysite or falls victim to Nestorianism. Critical theology considers the limitations of statements which are concerned with the fact of Jesus Christ. It prohibits the setting up of any statement on its own, and allows a statement only if it is qualified and supported by its contradictory opposite. Now this is already to have spoken of the thought forms in which theological thought takes place.

The whole thought of the ancient church was determined by the concept of *ousia*, nature, essence. It lies at the heart of christological thought. Liberal theology thought that the introduction of this concept into christology had Hellenized the gospel understanding of Jesus Christ and thus corrupted it. Against liberalism, it must be said that in its own way there is no thought-product less Greek than the Chalcedonian Definition. *Ousia* in the ancient church is not to be thought of in the light of the thought pattern which opposes nature and ethos (Ritschl). *Ousia* here really means the nature of God, the fact itself, the totality of God or the totality of man. The mistake lies elsewhere. It does not lie in the way in which the *ousia* concept had changed the moral understanding into a physical one, but in the way in which the nature of God and the nature of man were spoken of in a theoretical, objectifying way, so that these natures were regarded as two entities, distinguishable from each other, which afterwards come together in Jesus Christ. But the relationship between God and man cannot be imagined as a relationship of entities; it can only be thought of as a personal relationship. Moreover, nothing can be known of either God or man before God has become man in Jesus Christ. The advantage of the concept of *ousia* over a dynamic understanding of the incarnation (Paul of Samosata) lies in the *a priori* universalist conception of salvation which this concept implies. As a result, the reality of salvation can be described otherwise than in the latter approach, where everything depends on the dynamic act of will on the man's part, and the nature undergoes a process of divinization. The dynamic approach also begins with two separate substances and does not obviate the difficulty. It postulates and constructs the God-man from the prior knowledge of two isolated substances instead of taking as its presupposition the prior fact of the God-man.

This last course is the result of critical christology. Objectifying thought-forms, whether dynamic or concerned with the natures, are finally rejected and eliminated. By pointing to the fact itself, critical christology excludes these thought-forms. Only in the light of the fact itself can one know who God is. The contribution of critical christology can be summed up in three notions:

a. In the Chalcedonian Definition an unequivocally positive, direct statement about Jesus Christ is superseded and split into two expressions which stand over against each other in contradiction.

b. Objectifying thought succeeds in negating itself because it comes up against its own limitations. It comes to an end where its contradictory opposite must necessarily be recognized at the same time as itself. The recognition of this end makes room for what is plainly factual.

c. The question 'How?' succeeds in making itself impossible simply in the asking. It is directly connected with objectifying thought. Objectifying thought takes the question 'How?' out of itself, but it cannot answer the question of how the union of God and man is achieved. If the question 'How?' is consistently and relentlessly put to Christ, the result will be the Chalcedonian Definition, in which the question 'How?' has made an end of itself. All that remains is a pointer to the question 'Who are you?' The Chalcedonian Definition is itself ultimately the question 'Who?'

No christology can ever go back on these results. But what form is a positive christology to take on the basis of critical christology?

IV. POSITIVE CHRISTOLOGY

1. The Incarnate

The question may not run, 'How is it possible to conceive of the Incarnate?', but 'Who is he?' He is not adopted by

God, and he is not clothed in human characteristics. He is the God who has become man as we have become man. He lacks nothing that is man's. There is nothing offered by this world or by men which Jesus Christ did not take. The protest against *enhypostasia* must be maintained. Jesus Christ had his own human individual hypostasis and human mode of existence. The man that I am, Jesus also was. Of him alone is it really true that nothing human remained alien to him. Of this man we say, 'This is God for us.'

This does not mean that we know, say, at an earlier stage, quite apart from Jesus Christ, what and who God is, and then apply it to Christ. We have a direct statement of identity; whatever we can say here is prompted by a look at him, or, better, is compelled by this man. Neither does it mean that the statement 'This man is God' adds anything to his manhood. That is the essential point. *Per contra*, it could be argued that something was added to the man Jesus that we do not have, namely Godhead. And this is right. But we must be careful here. The union of God and man in Christ is not to be conceived of in terms of essence or *ousia*. The Godhead of Jesus is not an extension of his manhood. Nor is it something contiguous to his manhood, which Jesus goes on to achieve. The statement 'This man is God' touches on Jesus vertically from above. It takes nothing from him and adds nothing to him. It simply qualifies the whole man Jesus as God. It is God's judgment and Word on this man. But this qualification, this judgment and Word of God which 'comes from above' is in turn not to be thought of as something which is added. Rather than being understood as an addition, this Word of God coming from above is in fact the man Jesus Christ himself. And because Jesus Christ *is* also God's judgment on himself, he points at the same time both to himself and to God.

An attempt is thus made to avoid the union of two

demonstrable, isolated entities. Jesus, the man, is believed in as God. And he is believed in as the man, and not despite his manhood, or in addition to it. Faith in the Word ignites in the man Jesus. Jesus Christ is not God in a divine *ousia*; he is not God in a demonstrable and describable way; he is God in faith. There is no such thing as this divine essence. If Jesus Christ is to be described as God, then we may not speak of this divine essence, of his omnipotence and his omniscience, but we must speak of this weak man among sinners, of his cradle and his cross. When we consider the Godhead of Jesus, then above all we must speak of his weakness. In christology one looks at the whole historical man Jesus and says of him, 'He is God.' One does not first look at a human nature and then beyond it to a divine nature; one meets the one man Jesus Christ, who is fully God.

The accounts of the birth and the baptism of Jesus stand side by side. The birth points wholly to Jesus himself. The baptism points to the Holy Spirit coming from above. The difficulty of taking the birth narrative and the baptism narrative together is a consequence of the doctrine of the two natures. But the two accounts are not a doctrine of two natures. If we disregard this doctrine, the one story deals with the presence of the Word of God in Christ and the other with the descent of the Word of God on Jesus. The child in the cradle is the whole God; see Luther's christology in the Christmas hymns. The call at the baptism is a confirmation of the first event; there is no adoptionism in it. The cradle shows the man who is God, the baptism shows in respect of Jesus the God who calls.

So if we speak of Jesus Christ as God, we may not speak of him as the representative of an idea of God who possesses the properties of omniscience and omnipotence (there is no such thing as this abstract divine nature!); we must speak of his weakness, of the cradle and the cross; and this man is no abstract God.

Strictly speaking, we should really talk, not about the Incarnation, but only about the Incarnate One. An interest in the incarnation raises the question 'How?' The question 'How?' thus underlies the hypothesis of the Virgin Birth. It is both historically and dogmatically questionable. The biblical evidence for it is uncertain. If the biblical evidence gave decisive evidence for the real fact, there might be no particular significance in the dogmatic obscurity. The doctrine of the Virgin Birth is meant to express the incarnation of God and not just the fact of the Incarnate One. But does it not miss the decisive point of the incarnation by implying that Jesus has *not* become man wholly as we are? The question remains open, just as and just because it is already open in the Bible.

The Incarnate One is the glorified God. 'The Word was made flesh and we beheld his glory.' God glorifies himself in man. That is the ultimate mystery of the Trinity. The humanity is taken up into the Trinity; not since eternity, but 'from now to all eternity'. The glorification of God in the flesh is now at the same time the glorification of man, who is to have life with the trinitarian God for eternity. So it is incorrect to see the incarnation of God as a judgment of God on man. God remains the Incarnate One even at the last judgment. The incarnation is the message of the glorification of God who sees his honour in being man. It must be observed that the incarnation is primarily a real revelation of the creator in the creature, and not a veiled revelation. Jesus Christ is the unveiled image of God.

The incarnation of God may not be thought of as being derived from an idea of God where, say, the manhood already belongs to the idea of God, as in the case of Hegel. The biblical testimony, 'We saw his glory', is meant here.

If the incarnation is thus regarded as the glorification of God, we may not go on again to slip in a speculative idea of God, which derives the incarnation as necessary from the idea of God. A speculative basis for the doctrine of the incarnation in an idea of God would pervert the free relationship between the creator and the creature into a logically necessary one. The incarnation is contingent. God freely binds himself to the creature, and freely glorifies himself in the Incarnate. Why does that sound strange and improbable? Because the revelation of the incarnation in Jesus Christ is not a visible glorification of God. Because this Incarnate One is also the Crucified.

2. The Humiliated One and the Exalted One

In considering humiliation and exaltation, we are not investigating the divine and human natures, but the way God exists as man. We do not know a Godhead and a manhood each in its own nature. We are concerned with the way in which the one who has been made man exists. Thus 'humiliation' does not mean a state where the Incarnate One is more man and less God, in other words a stage in the limitation of God. Neither does exaltation mean a state where he is more God and less man. In humiliation and exaltation, Jesus remains fully man and fully God. The statement 'This is God' must be made of the Humiliated One in just the same way as it is made of the Exalted One.

We say of the Humiliated One, 'This is God.' He makes none of his divine properties manifest in his death. On the contrary, all we see is a man doubting in God as he dies. But of this man we say, 'This is God.' Anyone who cannot do this does not know the meaning of 'God became man'. In the incarnation, God reveals himself without concealment. Not the Logos, the Godhead or the manhood of Christ, but the whole person of the God-man is in the humiliation. He veils himself in the concealment of this scandal. The principle of the humiliation is not Christ's humanity but the 'likeness of flesh' (Rom. 8.3). With the exaltation, this is done away with, but Christ's manhood remains eternal.

The question is no longer, *How* can God be humiliated man? but rather, *Who* is the humiliated God-man? The doctrine of the incarnation and the doctrine of the humiliation must be strictly distinguished from each other. The mode of existence of humiliation is an act of the Incarnate. That does not, of course, mean that he can be separated in time from the act of the incarnation; the God-man in history is always already the humiliated God-man, from the cradle to the cross.

In what way is this special mode of existence of the humiliation expressed? In the fact that Christ takes sinful flesh. The humiliation is made necessary by the world under the curse. The incarnation is relative to the first creation, the humiliation to fallen creation. In the humiliation, Christ enters the world of sin and death of his own free will. He enters it in such a way as to hide in it in weakness and not to be known as God-man. He does not enter in the royal clothes of a 'Form of God'. The claim which he raises as God-man in this form must provoke antagonism and hostility. He goes incognito as a beggar among beggars, as an outcast among the outcast, despairing among the despairing, dying among the dying. He also goes as sinner among the sinners, yet in that he is *peccator pessimus* (Luther), as sinless among the sinners. And here the central problem of christology lies.

The doctrine of the sinlessness of Jesus is not one *locus* among others. It is a central point on which all that has been said is decided. The question runs: Did Jesus, as the humiliated God-man, fully enter into human sin? Was he a man with sins like ours? If not, was he then man at all? If not, can he then help at all? And if he was, how can he help us in our predicament, as he is in the same predicament?

It is vital here to understand what the 'likeness of flesh' can mean. It means the real image of human flesh. His flesh is our flesh. Liability to sin and self-will are an essential part of our flesh. Christ became involved in the predicament of the whole flesh. But to what extent does he differ from us? In the first place, not at all. He is man as we are, he is tempted on all sides as we are, indeed far more dangerously than we are. In his flesh, too, was the law that is contrary to God's will. He was not the perfectly good man. He was continually engaged in struggle. He did things which outwardly sometimes looked like sin. He was angry, he was harsh to his mother, he evaded his enemies, he broke the law of his people, he stirred up revolt against the rulers and the religious men of his country. He entered man's sinful existence past recognition.

But everything depends on the fact that it is *he* who took the flesh with its liability to temptation and self-will. *He* did this and that, which seem to the onlooker to be sin and failure, and must be evaluated as such. Because it is *he*, these statements, of course, appear in a different light. It is really human flesh that he bore—but because *he* bears it, this flesh is robbed of its rights. He pronounces the verdict on his action. He has anguish as we do; it is his anguish. He is tempted as we are; it is his temptation. He is condemned as we are, but because *he* is condemned, we are saved through him. In the light of this 'He' the harshest and most scandalous expressions about this humiliated God-man must be ventured and tolerated. He was really made sin for us, and crucified as the *peccator pessimus*. Luther says that he is himself robber, murderer and adulterer as we are, for he bears our sin, and in so doing describes the ultimate foundation of all christological statements. As the one who bears our sin, and no one else, he is sinless, holy, eternal, the Lord, the Son of the Father.

There can be no balancing of the two expressions 'sinner' and 'sinless', as though one could still separate the Humiliated One from the likeness of flesh. He is fully man; he gives the law its due and is judged, *and* robs sin of its force. He is completely in the likeness of flesh and under condemnation as we are, and yet he is without sin. The likeness of flesh with its realm of sin is related to him, but it is related to him, who is yet without sin. Without reaching an equilibrium we must say: *He*, not the likeness of flesh, is without sin; but he does not will to be distinguished from this likeness of flesh. Christology cannot get round this paradox.

The assertion of the sinlessness of Jesus fails if it has in mind observable acts of Jesus. His deeds are done in the likeness of flesh. They are not sinless, but ambiguous. One can and should see good and bad in them. If a man wishes to be incognito, one insults him if one says to him: I have both seen you and seen through you (Kierkegaard). So we should not justify Jesus' sinlessness by his actions. The assertion of the sinlessness of Jesus in his actions is no demonstrable moral judgment but a statement of belief that it is *he* who does these ambiguous actions, *he* who is eternally without sin. Faith acknowledges that the One who is tempted, is the victor, the One who struggles is the Perfect One, the Unrighteous One is the Righteous One, the Rejected, the Holy One. Even the sinlessness of Jesus is incognito, 'Blessed is he who is not offended in me' (Matt. 11.6).

The humiliated God-man is a stumbling block for the Jews, i.e. for the pious man. His historical ambiguity is a stumbling block. The pious man, the righteous man does not act as *he* did. The claim which this man raises, that he is not only a pious man but the Son of God, is incomprehensible to the pious man because it breaks every law: 'The men of old have said . . . but I . . .' The authority he assumes is incomprehensible: 'But I say to you' (Matt. 5.21), and 'Your sins are forgiven you' (Matt. 9.2). That is the essence of the scandal. Were Jesus not wholly man, but of a divinized nature, the claim might well have been allowed. Had he done the signs which were demanded of him for proof, men would probably have believed in him. But just when it came to the point of signs and wonders, he retreated into his incognito and refused to give any visible attestation. In this way he makes a stumbling block. But everything depends on this. Had he answered the question put to him about his authority with a miracle, then it would not be true that he was wholly man as we are. At the decisive moment, in the question about Christ, the exception would have been made. So the nearer the revelation, the thicker the concealment must be; the more urgent the question about Christ, the more impenetrable the incognito.

That means that the form of scandal is the very one which makes belief in Christ possible. In other words, the form of humiliation is the form of the *Christus pro nobis*. In this form Christ means and wills to be for us in freedom. Had Christ proved himself by miracles, we would 'believe' the visible theophany of the Godhead, but it would not be belief in the *Christus pro me*. It would not be inner conversion, but acknowledgement. Belief in miracles is belief in a visible epiphany. Nothing happens in me if I assert my belief in miracles. There is only faith where a man so surrenders himself to the humiliated God-man as to stake his life on him, even when this seems against all sense. Faith is where the attempt to have security from something visible is rejected. In that case, it is faith in God and not in the world. The only assurance that faith tolerates is the Word itself which comes to me through Christ.

Anyone who looks for signs of verification remains by himself. He is not changed. Anyone who recognizes the Son through the scandal is a believer in the New Testament sense. He sees the *Christus pro nobis*, he is reconciled and made new. The stumbling block in the incognito and the ambivalent form of the *Christus pro nobis* is at the same time the unceasing temptation of faith. The temptation, however, teaches us to pay heed to the Word (Isa. 28.19). And from the Word comes faith.

How are we to understand the fact that Jesus nevertheless does miracles? Are they not a breaching of the incognito? If the incognito has once slipped, is it not all a mockery? Are we, with liberal theology, to regard miracle as a phenomenon of the age? Or must we not at least return to the doctrine of the two natures? Must we not recognize a *genus maiestaticum*? The miracles are no breaching of the incognito. The ancient religious world is full of miracle workers and healers. Jesus is not alone in this. The realm of miracle is not identical with the realm of God. True, the miracles may exceed normal everyday happenings, but they are only on another level within the created world. The concept which goes with miracle is not that of God, but that of magic. Magic remains within the world. If Jesus does miracles, he preserves his incognito within the magical picture of the world. It is not miracle which accredits him as the Son of God in the New Testament. On the contrary, his authority is taken to be demonic.

Only the believing community recognizes the approach

of the kingdom in the miracles of Jesus. It does not see only magic and false claims here. But the incognito is not done away with for the unbeliever. The unbeliever sees magic and an ambiguous world. The believer says, 'Here is the kingdom of God.' Our age no longer lives in a magical world, but it is still inclined to take miracle as an unequivocal manifestation of the divine. But miracle remains ambiguous if it happens, and it needs to be explained. It *is* explained by both believer and unbeliever. The believer sees in it the prelude to the divine action at the end of the world. He sees, bound up with the incognito, something of the glory of God. 'We saw his glory' (John 1.14). But the non-believer sees nothing.

The Humiliated One is present to us only as the Risen and Exalted One. We know that he is the God-man in incognito only through the resurrection and the exaltation. As believers, we always have the incognito as an already penetrated incognito, we have the child in the cradle as the one who is eternally present, the one laden with guilt as the Sinless One. But the converse must also be valid. We cannot get round the scandal by means of the resurrection. We have the Exalted One only as the Crucified, the Sinless One only as the one laden with guilt, the Risen One only as the Humiliated One. Were this not so, the *pro nobis* would be done away with, there would be no faith. Even the resurrection is not a penetration of the incognito. Even the resurrection is ambiguous. It is only believed in where the stumbling block of Jesus has not been removed. Only the disciples who followed Jesus saw the resurrection. Only blind faith sees here. They believe as those who do not see, and in this faith they see. 'Blessed are they who do not see and yet believe' (John 20.29).

Between humiliation and exaltation the historical fact of the empty tomb lies oppressively starkly. What is the significance of the account of the empty tomb before the account of the resurrection? Is it the decisive fact of christology? If it was really empty, then is Christ not risen and our faith vain? It seems as though our faith in the resurrection were bound up with the account of the empty tomb. Is our faith then in the last resort only faith in the empty tomb?

This is and remains a last stumbling block which the person who believes in Christ must accept in one way or the other. Empty or not empty, it remains a stumbling block. We are not sure of its historicity. The Bible itself reveals the stumbling block in showing how hard it was to prove that the disciples had not perhaps stolen the body. Even here we cannot evade the realm of ambiguity. We cannot get round it anywhere. Jesus has entered even the testimony of Scripture in the form of a stumbling block. Even as the Risen One, he does not break through his incognito. He only breaks through it when he returns in glory. Then the Incarnate is no longer the Lowly One. Then the decision over faith and unbelief has already been made. Then the manhood of God is really and only the glorification of God.

We know all this now only from our encounter with the Lowly One. The church goes its own way of lowliness with this Lowly One. It cannot strive for a visible confirmation of its way while it renounces itself at every step. But as the lowly church, it may not look at itself in vain conceit, as though its lowliness were visible proof that Christ was present there. Lowliness is no proof, at least it is not a proof that one can refer to. There is no law or principle here which the church has to follow; this is a fact, in short, God's way with the church. As Paul says of himself that he can be either exalted or lowly so long as it happens for the sake of Christ, so too the church can be exalted and lowly, so long as it follows Christ's way. This way is the enemy of the proud, whether they wrap themselves in purple robes or set the martyr's crown upon their heads. The church always looks only to the humiliated Christ, whether it be exalted or lowly.

It is not good if the church boasts of its lowliness too hastily. It is equally bad if it boasts of its power and influence too hastily. It is only good if the church humbly acknowledges its sins, allows itself to be forgiven and acknowledges its Lord. Every day it must receive the will of God afresh from Christ. It receives it because of the presence of the Incarnate, Lowly and Exalted One. Every day this Christ once again becomes a stumbling block for its own hopes and wishes. Every day it comes anew to the sentence, 'You will all be offended because of me' (Matt. 26.31), and every day it holds anew to the promise, 'Blessed is he who is not offended in me' (Matt. 11.6).

A third section was intended, entitled 'The Eternal Christ'. But there is no sign of it. The semester had ended.

Index

1. Biblical References

2. Names

INDEX

3. Subjects

INDEX

INDEX

INDEX